TRAVELLERS

CAPE VERDE

By
SUE DOBSON

Written by Sue Dobson
Original photography by Sue Dobson

Published by Thomas Cook Publishing
A division of Thomas Cook Tour Operations Limited.
Company registration no. 1450464 England
The Thomas Cook Business Park, Unit 9, Coningsby Road,
Peterborough PE3 8SB, United Kingdom
Email: books@thomascook.com, Tel: + 44 (0) 1733 416477
www.thomascookpublishing.com

Produced by Cambridge Publishing Management Limited
Burr Elm Court, Main Street, Caldecote CB23 7NU

ISBN: 978-1-84157-948-1

Series Editor: Maisie Fitzpatrick
Production/DTP: Steven Collins

Printed and bound in Italy by: Printer Trento

Cover photography: Front: © Robert van der Hilst/CORBIS; © Spila Riccardo/SIME-4Corners Images; © Spila Riccardo/SIME-4Corners Images
Back: © Spila Riccardo/SIME-4Corners Images; © Spila Riccardo/SIME-4Corners Images.

The paper used for this book has been independently certified as having been sourced from well-managed forests and recycled wood or fibre according to the rules of the Forest Stewardship Council.
This book has been printed and bound in Italy by Printer Trento S.r.l., an FSC certified company for printing books on FSC mixed paper in compliance with the chain of custody and on products labelling standards.

Contents

Introduction

Scattered across the Atlantic Ocean off the coast of West Africa, the archipelago of ten islands and eight islets that make up the Republic of Cape Verde lies about 450km (280 miles) from the coast of Senegal and 1,000km (620 miles) southwest of the Canary Islands. Nine of the islands are inhabited, and, as each one is significantly different from its neighbours, island-hopping is a rewarding experience.

West of Africa and east of Brazil, the Cape Verde islands offer a fascinating mix of landscapes and cultures. A touch of the tropics in the heart of the Atlantic, the seemingly endless days of sunshine and temperatures that seldom drop below 20°C (68°F) or rise above 30°C (86°F) make it a year-round destination, while the scenic variety within and between the islands gives visitors myriad opportunities to explore or simply laze.

Here are islands for the windsurfer and the walker, the scuba-diver and the sailor, the deep sea fisherman and the music lover. There are vistas of long white beaches lapped by turquoise and emerald seas, and mountains of such dramatic beauty they leave you breathless. Shifting dunes seem to have been lifted from the Sahara, steeply terraced hillsides erupt into endless shades of green, and vines are tended in the crater of a still active volcano. Dolphins and whales are regular visitors, and turtles slip ashore by night to lay their eggs on secret beaches.

Islands of surprises

Cape Verde's islands never cease to surprise. The miles of powdery sand beaches for which the flat, desert islands of Sal, Boavista and Maio are famed contrast with the black volcanic sands of mountainous Fogo and São Nicolau. São Vicente's barren, red brown landscape couldn't be more different from the lush green valleys of Santo Antão, which lie a mere 50-minute ferry ride away.

Little villages of low-built, Portuguese-style houses are painted in sunshine-bright colours; in the hills, traditional thatch and stone-built homes cling to vertiginous ledges. Most roads are cobbled, hand hewn from the rocky ground on which they lie. Of the main towns, busy Praia feels African, and lively Mindelo is distinctly European.

Cape Verde's European and African heritage is revealed most strongly on

Santiago, the largest of the islands and home to the country's capital, Praia. All the contrasting elements of the other islands seem to come together on Santiago, for it combines a coastline that's partly barren and partly beach, with an interior packed with craggy mountains and fertile green valleys. This is where Cape Verde's history began, with the first European city in the tropics and the slave trading that once made it rich.

Tourism of the future

Sal is at the centre of a tourism industry that is still very much in its infancy. Hotels and a collection of simple restaurants line the beachfront of Santa Maria village on its southern coast. This is the island that will change the most in the coming years. Most of its barren landscape has been sold for development, apartment blocks are rising, and resorts the size of small towns are taking shape. Boavista, too, is preparing for an expected influx of sun-and-beach visitors and property buyers.

Cape Verde has sun, sea and sand in abundance. Yet there is so much more for the visitor with an enquiring mind and a sense of adventure. The islands capture the imagination, while the warmth and friendliness of the people, encapsulated in the Crioulo word *morabeza*, meaning 'welcome', stay long in the memory.

A typical cobbled road running through the hills of Santiago

The land

This cluster of volcanic islands that erupted from beneath the Atlantic Ocean between around 15 million and 100,000 years ago is made up of seven mountainous and three flat islands, and a collection of rocky islets. Widely spaced in a roughly arrowhead formation and covering a total surface area of 4,033sq km (1,557sq miles), they lie amid 60,000sq km (23,200sq miles) of ocean between latitude 14°N and 18°N and longitude 22°W and 26°W.

Legend has it that when God had finished creating the world, the tiny crumbs he brushed from his hands fell to the ocean, scattering like pearls to form the islands of Cape Verde. While each island has its own distinct characteristics, all ten are volcanic in origin, erupting aeons ago from 'hot spots' under the earth's crust.

Sal is believed to be the oldest island, at least 15 million years, and some say 26 million. Looking at it today, weathered and eroded into flatness with only patches of surf-pounded volcanic black rock and the outline of its sunken crater visible in the salt flats of Pedra de Lume, it's hard to imagine that perhaps Sal once resembled Fogo, the youngest island with its perfect cone-shaped, and still active, volcano. Nature has not finished with this awesome youngster formed a mere 100,000 years ago, as an eruption in 1995 made clear.

Maps show the Cape Verde islands divided into two groups: the Barlavento (Windward) islands of the north, consisting of Sal, Boavista, São Vicente, Santo Antão, São Nicolau and the uninhabited Santa Luzia, and the Sotavento (Leeward) islands of the south, consisting of Santiago, Fogo, Maio and Brava. However, the archipelago seems to divide more easily into east and west, the flat and the mountainous.

Spectacular beaches and mountains

The most easterly of the islands, those closest to the African coast – Sal, Boavista and Maio – are predominantly flat and renowned for their long, white-sand, quite spectacular beaches. Boavista boasts sinuous dunes at the coast, while inland drifting dunes of Saharan sand create bands of shimmering white across the red rock landscape. Oases of date palms add to the archetypal desert image.

The seven mountainous islands present striking contrasts. Fogo, Santo Antão and Brava have their heads in the

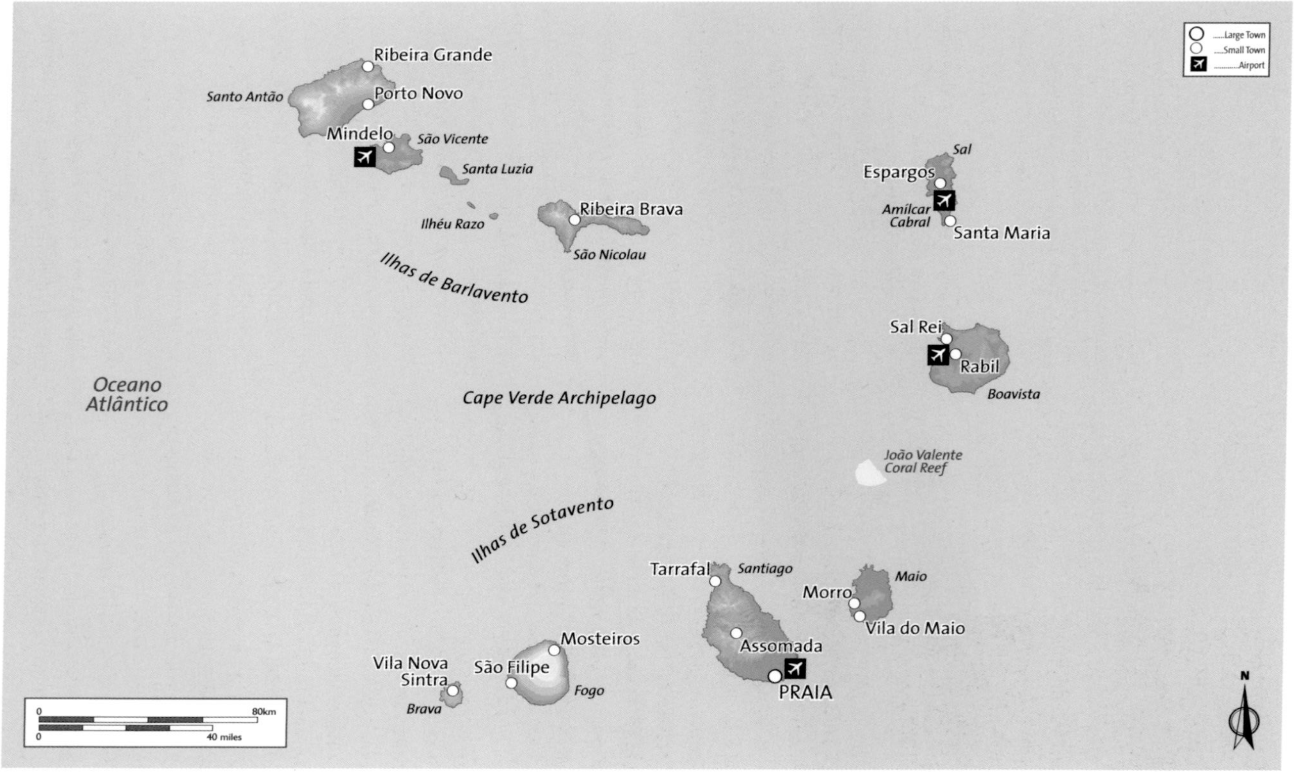

N
Large Town
Small Town
Airport
Ribeira Grande
Santo Antão
Porto Novo
Mindelo
São Vicente
Santa Luzia
Ilhéu Razo
Ribeira Brava
São Nicolau
Ilhas de Barlavento
Sal
Espargos
Amílcar Cabral
Santa Maria
Sal Rei
Rabil
Boavista
Oceano Atlântico
Cape Verde Archipelago
João Valente Coral Reef
Ilhas de Sotavento
Tarrafal
Santiago
Assomada
PRAIA
Maio
Morro
Vila do Maio
Mosteiros
São Filipe
Fogo
Vila Nova Sintra
Brava
0
80km
0
40 miles

clouds. Fogo's renowned peak rises to 2,829m (9,282ft), ringed by a crater that's 8km (5 miles) in diameter with walls on its western side towering to almost 1,000m (3,281ft). Amazingly, people live, work and farm within the black heart of the crater, tending vines and coffee plantations, making wines and exporting coffee beans. Nearby Brava, at 64sq km (25sq miles) the smallest of the inhabited islands, is frequently wreathed in a mist that waters gardens and bestows the title 'island of flowers'.

On Santo Antão there hardly seems to be an inch of flat land, so steep are its layers of craggy, cloud-piercing mountains and so deep its lush green valleys. Yet the drama and spectacle are all concentrated on the northeastern part of the island. The inaccessible, inhospitable west hasn't seen rain for years.

Most of São Nicolau is barren and bare, yet its mountainous heart is green and heavily cultivated, Sao Vicente's barren rocky landscape led the British to dub it 'the cinder heap', while tiny Santa Luzia, with a surface area of just 35sq km (13½sq miles) has little vegetation, peaks rising to 395m (1,296ft) and dune beaches, but no water to sustain human habitation. Santiago, in the southern group of islands, is a superb mix of rugged mountains, deep valleys layered with terraced fields, and a deeply indented coastline.

Drought and wind have shaped Cape Verde's landscapes and fortunes.

WATER

Lack of water is a serious problem in Cape Verde, a small country with few resources, where over a third of the population lives on less than €450 a year. To visitors staying in hotels and resorts with swimming pools and power showers, it seems inconceivable that many Cape Verdeans have to walk some distance, often up and down steep hills, to collect all the water the family needs for drinking, washing and cooking. Water from desalination plants, tankered to villages and small towns, is delivered to a central point that's usually open twice a day for two hours. The water collected has to be paid for and is expensive.

Northeast trade winds make their presence felt between December and April, and hot blasts of the sand-laden desert Harmattan wind can arrive between November and June. Climatically a marine extension of the Sahara, water, or lack of it, remains the biggest problem for the islands' inhabitants. In theory, the rainy season spans July to October; in reality, the showers may be sporadic, arrive in December, or not at all. Rain can fall on one part of an island, yet leave the rest untouched. A sudden, torrential downpour can cause dry riverbeds to flood, dislodge cobbled roads and wash the ever-decreasing topsoil seawards, despite impressively valiant attempts at terracing steep hillsides.

Planting trees

The seas are rich with fish, and the tropical underwater scenery is unique to the islands, quite different from that found off the West African coast or more distant Canary Islands. Cape Verde was never part of an ancient landmass, so whatever vegetation and birdlife that settled on the islands arrived by chance and evolved over the course of time. The grey-headed kingfisher, for example, is at home on walls and pylons on Santiago, far away from inland water. Small-leaved succulents creep across wind-whipped dunes on the desert islands; woody euphorbias frequent rocky soils.

Little is known of how the islands looked before human habitation in the mid 15th century, but early settlers reported using the wood of the fig tree in the construction of houses and boats, and judging by the number of places named Tarrafel, the tamarisk tree (*Tamarix senegalensis*), found at the mouths of coastal canyons, was once widespread. While there are still indigenous plant species, the natural vegetation of Cape Verde is sparse due to drought, erosion, the ravages of goats and poor farming practices.

The dragon tree (*Dracaena draco*) is one grand survivor, growing naturally in the higher reaches of São Nicolau and planted on Santo Antão and Santiago. Since independence, much has been done toward reforestation, with many millions of trees planted over the years. Oaks, pines, mimosa, sweet chestnut and eucalyptus thrive in the cool mountain air of Santo Antão, and sandy Maio is almost green with acacia trees. Conservation areas and national parks have been proclaimed – Cape Verde is fighting back after centuries of neglect.

Farms, fields and trees under Santo Antão's mountains

History

15 million years ago A volcano erupts from beneath the sea to create the island of Sal. Cape Verde is born.

100,000 years ago Fogo, the final volcanic island in the group, is formed.

1455–61 Cape Verde islands are discovered by Europeans. The southern Leeward islands are probably discovered by the Genoese mariner António de Noli, the northern Windward islands by the Portuguese explorer Diogo Afonso.

1462 The first Portuguese settlers arrive on Santiago and begin importing slaves from the west coast of Africa to cultivate the land.

1466 Authorisation to trade in slaves is received from Portugal.

1495 The Church of Our Lady of the Holy Rosary, the first permanent place of Christian worship in sub-Saharan Africa, is established in Ribeira Grande, Santiago. Cape Verde becomes a Portuguese Crown Colony.

1497 Portuguese navigator Vasco da Gama anchors off the island of Santiago and sails on a journey that will lead to the discovery of India.

1498 Christopher Columbus lands on Boavista, but isn't impressed.

1500s Ships from Portugal and Spain use Cape Verde as a supply station.

1533 Cape Verde's first town, Ribeira Grande (later renamed Cidade Velha) on Santiago, is so wealthy

A tiled picture showing Ponte Novo harbour on São Vicente in the late19th century

	and successful it is designated a city.
1541	Ribeira Grande is attacked by pirates.
1556	Building work begins on a cathedral at Ribeira Grande. It would take until 1693 before it was dedicated.
1578	Sir Francis Drake lands on the islands of Maio and Brava.
1580–83	The first of the great famines on the islands.
1585	Sir Francis Drake visits Cape Verde a second time, torching villages. His attacks the following year lead to the construction of a fort at Ribeira Grande.
1587	Portugal appoints a governor-general for Cape Verde and Guinea on the West African coast.
1600–1700s	Slave trading is at its lucrative height.
1620s	British ships begin calling at Maio and Sal to take on salt before fishing off Newfoundland. The salt trade would last for centuries.
1675–90	The 'monopoly years' in which Portugal severely restricts Cape Verdeans' trading rights.
1680	An earthquake and the eruption of Fogo's volcano force many people to flee the island. They settle on nearby Brava.
1712	French pirates sack Santiago and plunder its wealthy capital, Ribeira Grande.
1721	Portugal relaxes its monopoly rules and frees the Cape Verdeans to trade internationally.
1773–6	Drought decimates nearly half of Cape Verde's inhabitants.
1770	Praia on Santiago becomes the official capital of Cape Verde.
1802–82	The islands are used by Portugal to imprison convicts and dissidents.
1818	There are so many American merchant and whaling ships calling at the islands that a US Consul to Cape Verde is appointed.

1830s	Drought and famine kill over 30,000 people.
1832	Charles Darwin spends three weeks documenting the flora and fauna of Santiago.
1850s	Britain sets up coaling stations on São Vicente.
1854	Slave trading is officially abolished, but it continues.
1866	The San José Seminary, the first high school on the islands, opens in Ribeira Brava on São Nicolau.
1870	Britain establishes a transatlantic telegraph cable in São Vicente.
1900–1920s	Emigration of islanders to the United States increases.
1915	The first book of Cape Verdean poetry is published.
1921	Drought kills 17,000 people on São Vicente.
1936	Launch of *Claridade*, a journal publishing the work of local writers.
1939–45	Portugal garrisons soldiers on Cape Verde, resulting in anti-Portuguese sentiment among the drought- and hunger-stricken islanders.
1945	Cape Verde's worst drought period begins; 30,000 people die.
1949	Cape Verde's first airport opens on Sal.
1951	Cape Verde is defined by Portugal as an overseas province.
1956	The African Party for the Independence of Guinea and Cape Verde (PAIGC) is co-founded in Guinea-Bissau by Cape Verdean Amílcar Cabral.
1960	The liberation war against Portuguese rule in Guinea-Bissau begins, led by the PAIGC.
1969–75	Drought.
1973	Amílcar Cabral is assassinated.
1975	Cape Verde becomes an independent nation on 5 July. The president is the secretary-general of the PAIGC, Aristides Pereira, and the country is closely linked with Guinea-Bissau.

1980	A coup in Guinea-Bissau marks the end of the two countries' close ties.
1981	The PAIGC, the country's sole political party, is renamed the PAICV (African Party for the Independence of Cape Verde).
1987	*Odju d'Água* by Manuel Veiga, the first novel in the Cape Verdean Crioulo language, is published.
1990	Cape Verde becomes a multi-party democracy.
1991	First free presidential elections are held. The winner is António Mascarenhas Monteiro, supported by the recently formed Movimento para a Democracia (MpD), which wins the parliamentary elections and takes power, with its founder Carlos Veiga as prime minister.
1992	New flag and national anthem adopted.
2001	The PAICV regains control of government with a large majority. Pedro Pires is elected president.
2002	The government appeals for international food aid after the harvest fails.
2005	Praia's international airport opens on Santiago.
2006	The PAICV wins the elections again. Cape Verde hosts NATO 'Steadfast Jaguar' military exercises. Tourism to the islands increases 22 per cent over the year. The projection is for 1 million visitors annually by 2015. In November, the first direct flights from the UK to Cape Verde are introduced.
2007	The European Union grants Cape Verde 'Special Partner' status. China announces that São Vicente will become one of its five Special Economic Areas in Africa and promises further investment.
2008	New international airport on Boavista operational.
2009	The first Hotel Management School due to open in Praia.
2011	Next parliamentary and presidential elections.

The story of Cape Verde

Slavery, drought and emigration sum up the story of Cape Verde. From the earliest days after the archipelago was discovered and settlement began on Santiago and Fogo, slaves were shipped from countries on the coast of West Africa to farm and work the land. Once there were adequate numbers for the needs of the settlers, the lucrative business of slave trading began.

Strategically positioned between Europe, Africa and the Americas, Santiago proved the ideal place for ships to call for water, salt and provisions, and to purchase their human cargo. The Portuguese traders had done the hard work for them – they had got the slaves, taught them a few words of Portuguese, weeded out the sickly and dealt with the difficult. They had even baptised some of them. Slave merchants, relieved of the task of negotiating the treacherous creeks of the mainland where disease was rife, paid handsomely.

Droughts have affected the landscape of many islands

In populating the arid islands with goats to feed the ever-increasing number of ships calling in for supplies of salted meat, the already fragile ecosystem was irreparably damaged, leaving it open to the devastating effects of drought. As early as the 16th century there were reports of famine on Santiago. The 18th and 19th centuries saw poor rains, constant crop failures and high mortality across all the islands. In just six months of 1774, 22,666 died from famine on the archipelago. In 1830, 42 per cent of the population perished. In the 20th century too, cycles of drought and famine ravaged the islands. On São Vicente, 17,000 people died in 1921, 30,000 in 1945. Fogo and São Nicolau each lost a third of their populations in the

Abandoned houses on Boavista

drought of 1941–3. On Santiago, 65 per cent of the population died during the drought of 1946–8.

Lack of tree cover and poor farming methods were partly to blame for these disasters. Huge tracts of land, owned by a few rich men, were leased out in plots annually to subsistence farmers. If more crops were produced than the family needed, the excess was taken in rent. Consequently, there was no incentive for future planning in the years when the rains came.

For the desperate, poverty-stricken people of the islands, emigration was the only option. In the 19th century the whaling ships that called into tiny Brava took on crews of young men who settled in the whaling ports of New Bedford, Massachusetts and Newport, Rhode Island, starting an exodus that would see tens of thousands of Cape Verdeans emigrating in search of work.

Today there are more Cape Verdeans living outside the archipelago than on it. The biggest populations are in the USA, particularly Boston and New England, and in Portugal. There are communities across Europe, including the Netherlands, Spain, Italy, Luxembourg, Switzerland, Norway, Sweden and the UK, as well as in Brazil and Argentina. In Africa, Senegal, Gabon and the former Portuguese colonies of Guinea-Bissau, Angola and the islands of São Tomé and Principe are all home to many Cape Verdean people.

The ties to the Cape Verdeans' large extended families are strong and the remittances sent back to relatives on Cape Verde account for 10 per cent of its gross domestic product.

Politics

Independent since 1975, the Republic of Cape Verde is a politically stable, peaceful and democratic country. Multi-party elections for its 72-member National Assembly are held every five years. The president, too, is elected by popular vote.

At the last elections, in 2006, around 325,000 Cape Verde citizens were on the voting register. However, about 20 per cent of voters live abroad, most of them in Portugal.

Under Portuguese colonial rule from the 15th century until 1975, Cape Verde's ties with Portuguese Guinea in West Africa span a long history of slavery and slave trading. Trading monopolies granted to Cape Verde automatically included 'the Rivers of Guinea'.

The fight for independence

The PAIGC (African Party for the Independence of Guinea and Cape Verde) was formed by Cape Verdean Amílcar Cabral in 1956 (*see panel opposite*). Fighting began in Portuguese Guinea in 1963, starting a ten-year liberation war that saw the guerrilla tactics of the PAIGC demoralise and defeat the large Portuguese army, as similar movements were doing in other African countries under Portuguese rule. Some of the military officers defeated in Guinea, Mozambique and Angola formed the Armed Forces Movement that toppled the Lisbon regime in 1974. Cabral's belief that 'the destruction of Portuguese colonialism is what will destroy Portuguese fascism' proved correct.

Cabral was assassinated in 1973, a few months before the liberation of Guinea-Bissau. Luíz Cabral, Amílcar's younger brother, became its first president. Among those fighting in the forests of Guinea-Bissau were Aristides

A picture of Amílcar Cabral hanging in the Fundo das Figueiras Cultural Centre on Boavista

Pereira, who was to become the first president of Cape Verde, and Pedro Pires, its first prime minister.

Independence for Cape Verde did not come immediately, however. The country's strategic position on the crossroads between Europe, Africa and the Americas gave it a relevance Portugal was not keen to lose. America feared that Cape Verde might become a Soviet base. Yet political changes in Portugal led first to a transitional joint government and then, in June 1975, general elections. On 5 July, the newly independent Republic of Cape Verde was proclaimed, governed by the PAIGC.

A new country

Riddled by drought, depleted of natural resources and almost bankrupt, Cape Verde was in dire need of international aid. The socialist government used the tonnes of maize donated by the World Food Programme to pay the thousands of people who set about the construction of terraces and water-retention projects, planted trees in the battle against soil erosion, and broke stones to create pathways and roads. It invested heavily in education and health care.

In 1980, a coup in Guinea-Bissau severed the two countries' close ties, and in 1981 the PAIGC renamed itself the PAICV (African Party for the Independence of Cape Verde). It took another ten years before Party member Carlos Veiga formed the MpD (Movimento para a Democracia), leading to Cape Verde becoming a multi-party state. In January 1991, the first democratic elections were held, and the PAICV lost power to the MpD.

Veiga was prime minister until 2000, during which time the government cut public spending, began developing the fishing and tourism industries, and opened the country up to foreign investment. The PAICV swept back into power in 2001 and was re-elected in 2006.

With its policy of non-alignment, and a large diaspora due to mass emigration, Cape Verde has good relations with many countries, including Portugal. The nation's currency, the Cape Verdean escudo, is pegged to the euro. In November 2007, the country deepened its relationship with the European Union (EU) when it was granted EU 'Special Partner' status. Tourism, seen as crucial to Cape Verde's future development, is attracting huge amounts of foreign investment.

NATIONAL HERO

Born in 1924, Amílcar Cabral grew up in Guinea-Bissau and Cape Verde and was educated at the high school in Mindelo. Believing there was a political solution to the droughts and famine that had plagued his country, decimating its population, he went to Portugal to study agriculture. While working as an agronomist in Guinea, he developed the strategy for a national liberation movement and started the PAIGC (African Party for the Independence of Guinea and Cape Verde) in 1956. Fighting to end Portuguese colonialism began in 1963. He was assassinated in January 1973, just months before the war was won.

Culture

With their African and European roots, the people of Cape Verde have a vibrant cultural mix, speaking a language that is uniquely theirs, and enjoying a passion for music that excites the senses. Poetry and song are especially important in the islands.

A sense of nationhood came late to Cape Verde. It was only in the last century that Cape Verdeans began to value and celebrate their history and cultural identity. By instituting a seminary and secondary school, the Portuguese made Cape Verde the educational centre of its colonial outposts and, from its *mestiço* (mixed race) population, an educated elite emerged to act as middlemen and administrators.

In the early 20th century, the first stirrings of nationhood emerged from a group of writers, poets and journalists. In 1936 a literary journal, *Claridade*, was published, introducing the idea of 'Cape Verdeanness'. Slowly but surely people's life experiences, vibrantly expressed in their music, poetry and songs, finally came to be valued.

Music and dance

From the drumming of *batuque*, a dance and music genre rooted in Africa, and the processional *coladeira* performed at festivals, to the sensuous movements of *funaná* and the wistful, bittersweet *mornas* that tell of partings and longing, music and dance are the essence of life for Cape Verdeans. Wherever people gather there will be music, and all of it tells a story (*see pp62–3*).

Musicians in Mindelo, São Vicente

EDUCATION

High priority was given to education after independence and this continues today. Cape Verde now has one of the highest literacy rates in West Africa. Although tuition is free for the compulsory six years of primary education, textbooks, writing materials and uniforms have to be bought. This can be a drain on the finances of a large family, and the fees payable for high school can prove too much. Many gifted students study abroad on grants provided by the host countries.

Language and literature

Although Portuguese is the official language of Cape Verde, and the medium of teaching in schools, Crioulo (Creole) is the everyday language of the people. It goes back to the very beginnings of settlement on the islands when slaves, banned from speaking their own languages, had to learn to communicate with each other and with their owners. Crioulo has evolved down the centuries, and differs from island to island.

The earliest books by Cape Verdean authors were published in the late 19th century in Portuguese. A Portuguese style of poetry also emerged. In the 1930s, Jorge Barbarosa introduced the first true Cape Verdean poetry. Like the poetic words of the *morna* songs, it reflected the *sodade*, or longing, felt by people who have had to emigrate. In recent times, the renowned musician and poet Kaká Barboza has published several volumes of Crioulo poetry.

The classic *Chiquinho*, the first novel to have a Cape Verdean cultural theme and reflect life on the islands, appeared in 1947. It was written by Baltasar Lopes da Silva, a founding member of the literary *Claridade* movement. The first novel to be published in Crioulo, *Odju d'Água* by Manuel Veiga, was published in 1987 (*see pp74–5*).

Reflecting the nation

Unveiled in 1992, Cape Verde's flag reflects the people and their nation. It has two horizontal bands of dark blue, symbolising the infinite space of the sea and the sky that surround the islands, which are separated by a white stripe that stands for peace, and a central red stripe denoting the determination of the people in the face of adversity. A circle of ten yellow stars represents the islands that make up the archipelago.

Part of a mural in Mindelo, São Vicente, which celebrates the island's love of music

Festivals and events

Cape Verdeans love to celebrate and party until dawn. Most of the festivals are linked to Catholic saints' days, and incorporate the islanders' long tradition of music and dance. Each island has its Municipality Day when their patron saint is commemorated with processions and traditional food. Several music festivals have gained world renown, and Mindelo's Carnival is an event to remember.

February

World Wave Surfing Championships The surf's up on Sal, and Ponta Preta beach hosts these thrilling championships.

February/March

Every island celebrates on the day before Lent begins, but two of the carnivals are truly spectacular.

Mindelo's Carnival Exotic costumes and feathered headdresses, processions of extravagantly decorated floats, fun street theatre, drumming and dancing in the streets.

São Nicolau's Carnival Considered to have the most humorous carnival costumes, with colourful floats, powerful drumming and lively music.

April/May

Bandeira (Flag) de São Filipe Fogo's big celebration takes place at the end of April. *Coletcha*, a tradition in which women prepare the dish of *xerem* by pounding maize in a pestle to the rhythm of drums, is followed by jousting, the bearing of the flag to the church for its blessing, and singing and dancing by firelight. The following day there's Mass, a procession, horse racing, and much feasting.

Salvador do Mundo (Saviour of the World) Music Festival, Santiago Held at the end of April (*see p85*).

May

Gambôa Music Festival Santiago's festival is on Praia's Gambôa beach from 19 May. It runs for three nights, attracting local and international bands, and thousands of spectators.

Mass precedes the start of the music festival in Santa Maria das Dores on Sal

Island saints' days are celebrated with processions

June

São João Baptista, Santo Antão
All the islands celebrate the feast of São João (St John the Baptist) on 24 June, but on Santo Antão it's a major event. There a statue of the saint is carried on a 21km (13-mile) long procession. It is accompanied by drummers, dancers and people carrying palm branches. After Mass the partying begins.

São João, Brava Preparations for the feast on 24 June begin three days in advance with the pounding of maize in a pestle to make *xerem*. Bonfires are lit on the night of 23 June, a horseman carries the Cape Verdean flag to the church and fireworks light the night sky. The next day sees a procession, Mass, and more celebrations.

July

Santa Isabel, Boavista Saint Isabel is the patron saint of Boavista island and her day, 4 July, is celebrated in Sal Rei with a procession, a blessing of the sea, the decorating of homes with palm fronds, sporting events and partying.

August

Baía das Gatas Music Festival Held at the São Vicente beach over the weekend of August's full moon, this festival attracts international acts, local bands, and up to 100,000 people.

September

Mindelact: Mindelo International Theatre Festival For two weeks in September, São Vicente hosts this festival, which welcomes theatre groups from around the world and includes new Cape Verdean writing.

Sal's Music Festival This takes place on the beach at Santa Maria over a mid-month weekend and 20,000 people come to revel in the all-night sounds of popular local and international world music stars.

SCARING THE WITCHES

In the past it was believed that witches would try to harm a newborn baby. If they hadn't succeeded by the seventh night after the birth, the *noite-de-sete*, they'd turn into dangerous animals and roam above the house. Salt was spread on the roof and a great noise made throughout the night to see them off. Music, lots of food, *grogue* (a local spirit) and all-night partying did the trick, proving to the wicked witches just how well the baby was protected. The *noite-de-sete* is still part of the birth ritual, but today it's just a great excuse to celebrate royally.

Highlights

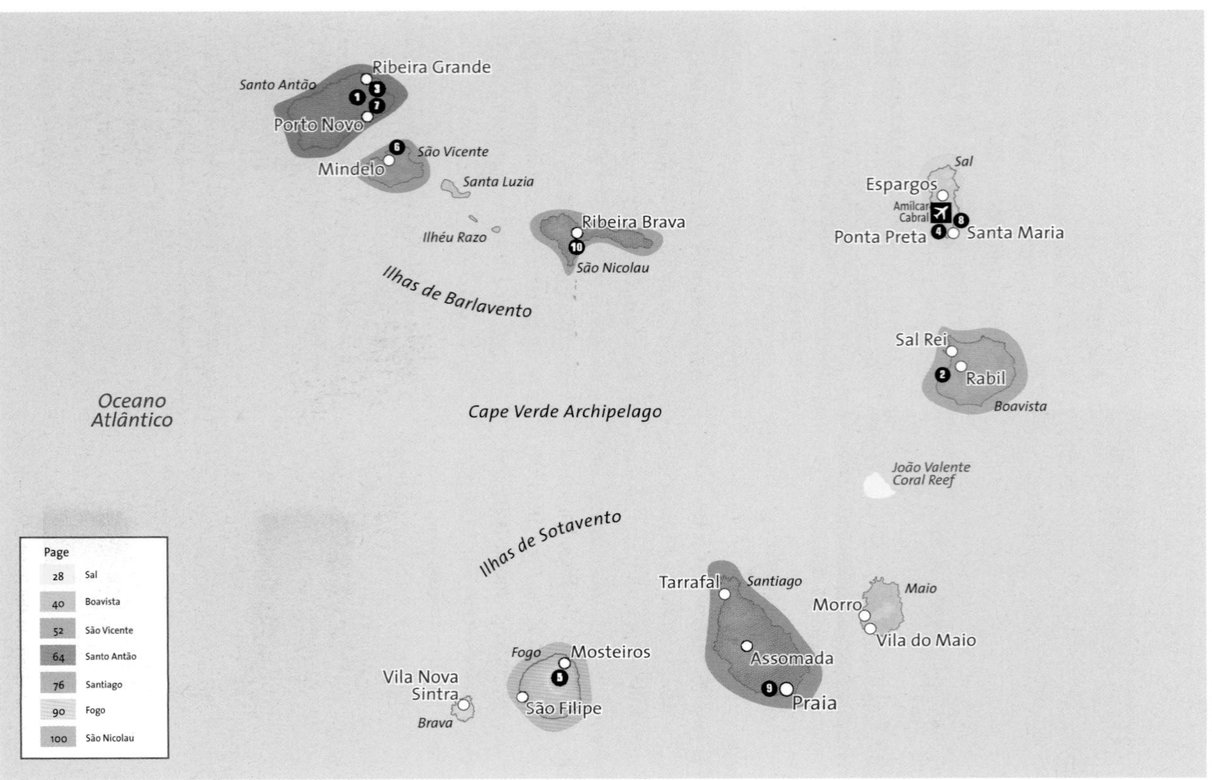
Santo Antão
Ribeira Grande
Porto Novo
São Vicente
Mindelo
Santa Luzia
Ilhéu Razo
Ribeira Brava
São Nicolau
Ilhas de Barlavento
Sal
Espargos
Amilcar Cabral
Ponta Preta
Santa Maria
Sal Rei
Rabil
Boavista
Oceano Atlântico
Cape Verde Archipelago
João Valente Coral Reef
Ilhas de Sotavento
Tarrafal
Santiago
Assomada
Praia
Maio
Morro
Vila do Maio
Fogo
Mosteiros
São Filipe
Vila Nova Sintra
Brava
Page
28 Sal
40 Boavista
52 São Vicente
64 Santo Antão
76 Santiago
90 Fogo
100 São Nicolau

1. **Santo Antão** Be thrilled by Santo Antão's spectacular mountain scenery on the route from Porto Novo to Ribeira Grande (*see pp64–73*).

2. **Boavista** Walk for miles along the almost deserted, wide and white-sand Chaves beach (*see p45*).

3. **Valleys and mountains on Santo Antão** Hike along the lush *ribeiras* (valleys) and terraced mountain slopes (*see p68*).

4. **Ponta Preta** Surf the big waves on Sal. Professionals rate it highly, placing Sal among the top five wind surfing destinations in the world (*see p36*).

5. **Fogo** Climb the Pico, Fogo's volcano cone, and trek in the crater among vineyards and fruit farms (*see pp90–94*).

6. **Mindelo** Hear local musicians play their haunting music in Mindelo, São Vicente (*see pp53–7*).

7. **Oxen on Santo Antão** See oxen drive a *trapiche*. This archaic contraption presses sugar cane to distil *grogue*, the local (highly alcoholic) drink (*see p70*).

8. **Santa Maria** Watch Sal fishermen wade ashore balancing huge fish on their heads, then deposit them in wheelbarrows for delivery to restaurants (*see pp31–3*).

9. **Praia** Visit Santiago's vibrant African market in Cape Verde's capital city (*see pp78–9*).

10. **São Nicolau** Discover rare and endangered dragon trees on their home island (*see p101*).

A mountain village in the heart of Santo Antão

Suggested itineraries

With nine very different islands to choose from, whether you have just a short time or the luxury of three weeks, you'll be spoilt for choice on Cape Verde. Relax on powdery white sand or try your hand at kite surfing, quad-biking or diving in the crystal clear waters. Hike in lush green valleys among fields of sugar cane and bananas, trek in high mountains – and discover long, deserted beaches where the only footprints in the sand will be yours.

Long weekend

If you have a few days to spare on Santiago, head for the cool of the mountains to chill out at the Pousada Quinta da Montanha (*see p156*). It's only 24km (15 miles) from the busy city of Praia and is surrounded by spectacular scenery right in the heart of the mountains at Rui Vaz. It's the sort of place where you can just put your feet up and take in the panoramic views, or take off to hike along paths on journeys of discovery. If you're feeling energetic, Pico de António, at 1,394m (4,574ft), the highest mountain on the island, is waiting to be climbed. At night, use the hotel's telescope to do some stargazing from the terrace.

For something completely different, fly to Fogo to spend a couple of nights at the Pousada Pedro Brabo (*see p157*) in the heart of the volcano

Rui Vaz's mountain setting, Santiago

The Pousada Pedro Brabo stands within the volcano crater on Fogo

crater. As well as hiking and climbing, you can visit the village, join locals in the bar and check out the wine *cooperativa* where there's often music and dancing.

From Mindelo, São Vicente, the island of Santo Antão is under an hour away by ferry and its dramatic landscapes are a paradise for hikers. Hiking maps are available and the choice of routes spans scenic valleys packed with sugar cane, banana plantations and exotic fruit trees, villages perched precariously on terraced hillsides, and towering craggy mountains.

The ferry docks in Porto Novo, from where it's about a two-hour drive in an *aluguer* (minibus taxi) along a zig-zagging road that follows bare brown hills into a magical, mountainous world of green, and down again to the coast at the town of Ribeira Grande. The *aluguer* drivers congregate at the dock gate, and are pretty vociferous, but when you book your accommodation check whether transport from the port can be arranged.

One week

Most international visitors arrive on flights into Sal, where there are beaches, water sports and the biggest selection of hotels in Cape Verde. It is also the most organised island for tourism, and many will stay here for their week's holiday.

Santa Maria on Sal's south coast is the setting for a collection of beachside hotels, from large all-inclusives providing plenty of organised entertainment to quieter establishments with good restaurants, as well as self-catering apartments. Spend your days soaking up the sun by the pool, walking on sandy beaches, trying out the variety of water sports, enjoying the seafood and checking out the little town's bars and small restaurants. A tour of the island won't take more than a morning.

As Sal has been designated for massive development – the home of the property boom – it will be a long time before all the building work finishes.

If the sun and the beaches have attracted you to the country, consider combining Sal with Boavista, a 25-minute flight away. Boavista has even better beaches than Sal and the red rock interior of the island is more interesting. Here you can see island life in small towns and villages of brightly painted houses, discover Saharan dunes and marvel at wide beaches of fine white sand, washed by a white-frothed cobalt sea, that stretch as far as the eye can see.

For a real contrast, combine Santiago with Sal. There are direct flights between the two islands, and the flying time is only about half an hour. Santiago is the biggest of the Cape Verde islands, home to the country's lively capital, Praia, and it has a bit of everything – history, bays and beaches, mountains, trees and terraced fields – and it is gloriously green after the rainy season.

Two weeks

In two weeks you can begin to truly experience Cape Verde's varied landscapes, and if you are curious by nature you will want to do some island-hopping. Bear in mind that tourism is very much in its infancy here, timetables can be flexible, and sometimes things don't go to plan. When you're sightseeing, bouncing around on cobbled roads in the heat can be tiring, so build some space and relaxation time into your itinerary.

Unwind after you arrive on the beaches of Sal or Boavista, then take off for a taste of Cape Verdean culture in Mindelo, São Vicente. Famed for being the home of musicians and poets, with its British and colonial Portuguese-style architecture, it's the most European of all the island towns. There are some good restaurants and bars with live music, especially at weekends, and the nightlife can be lively.

From Mindelo take the ferry across to Santo Antão and you won't believe how different two relatively close islands can be. While little can grow on São Vicente's stony ground, the northeast of Santo Antão is rich with vegetation. Layers of rugged mountains reach for the sky, and the deep valleys are unbelievably verdant. By taking the early morning ferry, it's quite possible to do the breathtakingly scenic drive across this part of the island in a day, returning to Mindelo in the early evening. However, staying on the island for a night or two will give you the opportunity to do some hiking and see the villages that perch in the mountains. There's accommodation in Ponta do Sol at the coast, but the rural retreat of Pedracin Village (*see p155*) has great mountain views.

From São Vicente fly to Santiago, which has a much more African feel, not surprising given that this island was the centre of the slave trade that filled the coffers of the Portuguese crown. Praia is a busy capital with a colourful, typically African market, while the centre of the island is beautifully mountainous and Tarrafal beach up in the north curves into a bay.

If you want to take in one more island, make it Fogo. A short flight from Santiago, the highlight here is the awesome volcano. Dark and brooding, its vast caldera holds surprises – it is home to two villages, a hotel and a wine cooperative.

Longer visits

With the luxury of a longer stay you can do all of the above, and more. Beach-lovers who are happy just to relax and aren't looking for entertainment will enjoy little Maio, which tourism had passed by until quite recently. Don't miss São Nicolau, where there's a splendid drive that takes you up into farming villages in the mountains and down to the black-sanded coast where the fishing community lands tuna by the ton and cans it (*see pp106–7*). It's a great island for hiking.

A view over Mindelo's bay, Porto Grande, to Monte Cara

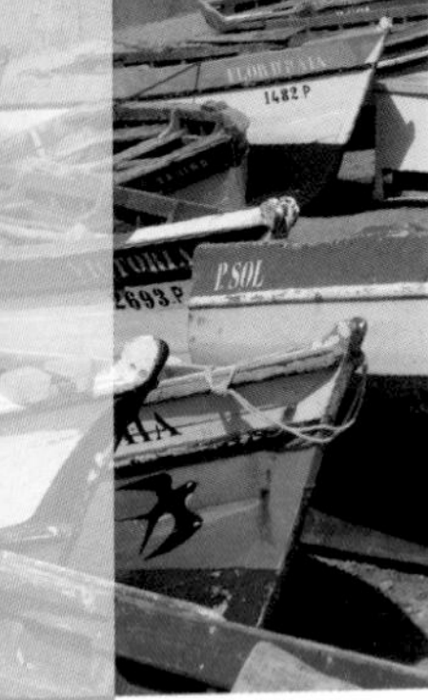

Sal

Named after the salt that was once extracted and shipped around the world, Sal is where tourism to Cape Verde started. For many years the only island with an international airport, it still receives the majority of the flights arriving from Europe and is the most visited of all the islands. Hotels line the 8km (5-mile) long sandy shore of Santa Maria das Dores, known simply as Santa Maria, where the sea is a glorious sapphire blue.

Initially, as your plane circles over the featureless, bare brown land, you may wonder what you've let yourself in for. Sal is an island of rocky plains and desert sand, its highest point the ambitiously named Monte Grande at 406m (1,332ft) in the northeast. Little grows on its flat, arid land and the few dusty acacia trees are bowed by the wind. After a 20-minute drive along a wide asphalt road south from the airport to Santa Maria, you see Sal's attractions – the beach, the sea and the hotels.

One of the easternmost islands of the archipelago, a member of the Barlavento (Windward) group, Sal is just 30km (18½ miles) long and 12km (7½ miles) at its widest, with a total surface area of 216sq km (83sq miles). Most of the population of 18,000 lives in Espargos, the main town near the airport, in the centre of the island. About 3,500 people live in the village of Santa Maria, on the south coast. With its construction boom of holiday villas, apartments and resort developments, Sal is attracting workers from other islands.

Sal is for beach-lovers and water-sports enthusiasts, for eating fish fresh from the sea and for lazing in the sun by the hotel pool.

A brief history

Although Sal was probably discovered in the 15th century – some say it was found before that by Moors from the African coast, although they left no traces – its barren landscape and lack of water meant it was only used by a few farmers for the raising of goats, and possibly some slaves working on the extraction of salt. Its original name was Llana, meaning 'Flat'. Yet the abundance of salt both changed its name and brought the island to life when Manuel António Martins arrived at the turn of the 19th century and set up his salt extraction and export business at Pedra de Lume.

You can see some of Santa Maria's old salt flats, abandoned now, on the

Sal (see pp36–7 for orange route drive)

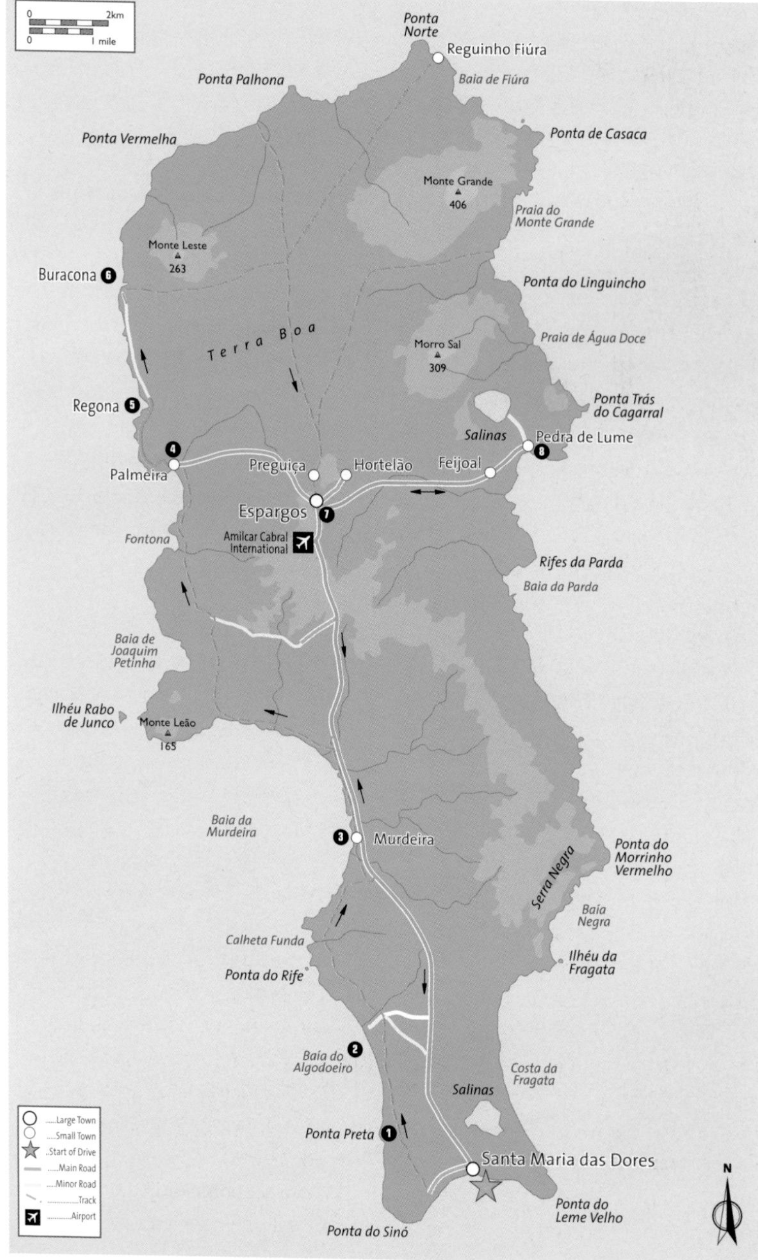

outskirts of the village. They were the reason Santa Maria was founded in 1830, and the wooden jetty on the beach, which was rebuilt in 2007, is where the salt was loaded onto ships destined for Africa and Brazil. There's a replica of one of the old wooden pumps used in the salt extraction process in the centre of Santa Maria's main square.

That Sal has an international airport was due firstly to the Italian dictator Benito Mussolini, who needed a refuelling point for aircraft flying between Europe and South America during World War II. Portugal sold the Italian leader the right to build an airport on Sal, and in 1945 bought back the site, which it developed. Then during the Apartheid years, when South African planes were refused landing rights in African countries, Portugal again provided a safe refuelling base on its Cape Verde island.

Santa Maria's first hotel, an extension in the grounds of the winter home of Belgian businessman Gaspard Vynckier and his wife Marguerite, was created in the 1960s to house South African Airways' crews on stopovers. Seconds from the beach, the Hotel Morabeza has grown into one of Santa Maria's finest hotels, and is still managed by a member of the Vynckier family, the original owners' granddaughter, Sophie (*see p148*).

The view along Santa Maria beach

Unloading a mackerel catch in Santa Maria

Santa Maria das Dores

With its long, long beach of fine sand, and a translucent sea of mesmerising blue and turquoise, Santa Maria is home to some of the best hotels in Cape Verde. It certainly has the biggest selection. A collection of bars, small shops and a clutch of simple but good restaurants line the three wide, cobbled streets that back the eastern end of the beach. Behind and around them are dusty streets of low-built houses, some of them brightly painted, where the residents live with few luxuries. The village has a school, a church, a community centre and a much-appreciated football stadium.

There's plenty of activity along the wooden jetty when fishermen land their catch around midday. The boats are small, but the sea is so rich in tuna, wahoo, garoupa and horse mackerel that their arrival is always worth watching. Men hoist the big fish such as tuna and sailfish onto their heads before depositing them in waiting wheelbarrows, then they trundle off in the direction of nearby hotels and restaurants.

The jetty is also where *Neptunus*, Sal's 'yellow submarine', sets out for two shipwrecks off the coast and for views of the fishy underwater universe from its glass-bottomed viewing chamber. If you're lucky you may see schools of dolphins leaping and diving nearby.

Santa Maria's main beach stretches west of the pier and is where most of

A fisherman with his catch of tuna

the big hotels are situated, culminating in a massive 1,000-roomed all-inclusive complex in Moroccan-style architecture that's about a 25-minute walk or short taxi ride from Santa Maria village.

The sea can be warm and temptingly calm but, depending on the wind, the waves can also crash ashore and have an undertow. There are no lifeguards, so it's wise to check conditions carefully before swimming.

Water sports are the main activities in Santa Maria. Windsurfing is particularly popular and there are several centres for the hire of equipment. There are good diving schools, too, and a variety of sites for scuba-diving, from reefs and shipwrecks to canyons and tunnels. Well-equipped boats are available for half-day or full-day fishing trips, with the option of bottom fishing for sea bream, garoupa and redfish, or game fishing for tuna, dorado (dolphin fish), wahoo and sailfish, even the highly prized blue marlin (*see p151*). For landlubbers, quad-biking in the low dunes is fun and can be arranged in guided groups from most hotels.

Windsurfers and kite surfers achieve good speeds blasting across the flat water off Santa Maria's main beach. For wave riders, the swell gets stronger at the far end of the bay. The northeast trade winds that blow between October and June are at their strongest from

December to February, often reaching 24 knots, which is when thrill seekers head for the bay at Ponta Preta, just up the west coast from Santa Maria's major property and resort developments.

Ponta Preta is rated among the world's top windsurfing locations, so good that several well-known wave riders, including former world champions, have made Sal their home. The prestigious Trilogy Windsurfing Competition is held here and Ponta Preta hosted one leg of the World Windsurfing Championships for the first time in 2007. Waves can reach 2.5m (8ft).

Music fans should plan to be in Santa Maria around 15 September, the village's Municipality Day, when a two-night Music Festival on the beach attracts international world music stars alongside great local bands, who play through to dawn and beyond.

Pedra de Lume

The salt pans that brought brief prosperity to Sal lie at the base of the vast sunken crater of a long extinct volcano on the east of the island. They are reached through a tunnel, which took slaves three months to hack out of the rock. Before the tunnel was built, laden donkeys would climb up the volcano slopes and down the other side to reach the port. In 1919 a French company installed a pulley system that enabled them to shift 25 tonnes of salt an hour. The wooden frames that march down the hill to the old port are rickety now, but they give an idea of how the system worked. A small amount of salt is still extracted from the area, for local consumption.

Separated by stone 'walls', the huge salt pans are an extraordinary sight, shimmering in a variety of shades of blue, pink and crusty white against a backdrop of brown volcanic hills. They form one of the few wetland areas in Cape Verde and are a good place to see birdlife. A variety of waders strut in a shallow lagoon, including the red-legged, black-winged stilt (*Himantopus himantopus*). Pedra de Lume is its last remaining breeding site in Cape Verde.

At the foot of the road leading down into the salt pans, there are changing rooms and showers for those who fancy immersing themselves in the grey volcanic mud that is said to be good for the skin and for easing various bodily aches and pains, or for those who want to float in the heavy saltwater pools.

JUST BEING FRIENDLY?

The young men who hassle tourists outside hotels and in the centre of Santa Maria are not locals (Cape Verdeans don't do that) but traders from West Africa, usually from Senegal and Guinea-Bissau. They are not threatening, just trying hard to do a job, but they can be irritating. They begin by trying to engage you in conversation, guessing where you're from, and then hope you'll go along with them to their 'workshop' to buy woodcarvings. If you're not interested in doing that, it's best not to get talking. A smile and a firm 'No, thank you' as you keep on walking usually does the trick.

Salt pans fill the crater of a long-extinct volcano at Pedra de Lume

The old village of Pedra de Lume, a couple of rows of tiny houses with colourfully painted doors but no amenities looking out onto a fishing bay, has a primary school and a 19th-century chapel. Ildo Lobo, one of Cape Verde's most popular musicians, grew up here. The occupants are to be rehoused, possibly in 2008, to make way for a huge property development: a resort with villas, apartments, bars, restaurants, an 18-hole golf course and a marina and yacht club.

On 15 August, a religious festival brings people from all over the island to Pedra de Lume's white-painted, blue-windowed chapel, built in 1853, where a statue of Nossa Senhora de Piedade (Our Lady of Mercy) is central to the celebrations. As well as a procession and Mass, the festival includes sporting activities and a small music festival.

Espargos

Named after a wild asparagus plant that used to grow on the sandy soil, Sal's rapidly expanding commercial and administrative centre has banks and offices, some cafés, restaurants and small shops and, in the big new residential suburbs, a smart football stadium and large high school.

The old part of Espargos has streets of yellow- and pink-painted houses, women sell fruit and vegetables from pavements, and men play cards and board games under the shade of trees that decorate the little square. It's worth a wander to glimpse daily life in the island's only real town.

Palmeira

Everything on Sal has to be imported, and Palmeira, the island's port, is busy with the unloading of ships. It has large storage facilities, a desalination plant – lack of fresh water is a serious problem on Sal – and an electricity station that serves the whole island. The little town is made up of low, brightly painted Portuguese-style houses, and locals gather under the shade of a big tree by the harbour to talk and play music. Just outside town, a small oasis of palm trees reveals how Palmeira got its name.

Buracona

On the northwest coast, where frothing surf pounds black volcanic lava rock, Buracona (Big Hole) is a popular diving spot. The 'blue eye' is a deep pool above a cavern which, when sunlight hits the right spot, provides a dazzling show of turquoise and blue as sunbeams pierce the clear water and dance on the cave floor far below. It doesn't look the ideal place for a swim, but there's a big pool of calm water in the heart of the rock, framed by jagged peaks that form a barrier against the crashing surf.

Waves crash against the rocks at Buracona, but sheltered pools attract divers and swimmers

Drive: Sal

Much of this route is on rough and sandy terrain, so you'll need a four-wheel-drive vehicle. It's important to follow existing tracks, and local advice is to take two cars when going off the main roads. Alternatively, hire a car and driver.

See map on page 29 for route.

The drive is 25km (15½ miles) and makes a half-day excursion, longer if you like walking on deserted beaches or plan to try floating in Pedra de Lume's salt lagoons.

Leave Santa Maria just before the main road to Espargos, to the left opposite Pirata disco. This route passes hotel entrances. At the Crioula Hotel go right and continue past the Riu complex.

1 Ponta Preta

Just past the Riu, look for tracks in the sand to your left and head for the surfer's favourite beach, Ponta Preta. In summer the water in the bay looks calm, but winter winds whip up impressive waves.

Drive northwards across stony desert, following the coast, and when the track splits take the left fork to Baía do Algodoeiro.

2 Baía do Algodoeiro (Algodoeiro Bay)

The water is a blissful blue and turquoise, and the bay curves gently towards the distinctive outline of Lion's Head in the distance. Past the Paradise Beach development, well-rutted tracks take you close to the waves. You'll pass an isolated farm and then the Cadjitinha fish restaurant perched above beaches where turtles lay their eggs. The owners rescue small turtles that have become stranded on rocks along their route to the sea. The views are of deserted beaches, low dunes and white-crested waves.

At Calheta Funda beach, the track bears right and again follows the bay. About 8km (5 miles) from Ponta Preta, you meet up with the main road to Espargos at a roundabout. Take the old road, now a track, that runs parallel with this towards Murdeira.

3 Murdeira

Murdeira was the site of the first major development of villas and apartments. Beyond Baía Village Club, take the track on the left that follows the coast, crossing flat brown desert and gentle dunes. It heads inland to climb a stony hill, with panoramic views from the top.

Fontona, a creek lined with green trees, appears to the left, before you dip down into a small oasis of palms and acacia trees, sadly spoiled by litter.
Drive past the oil terminal and houses to enter Palmeira.

4 Palmeira

Sal's port is home to about 1,100 people. Take a walk along the narrow streets of brightly painted houses, join locals in the cobbled square, where children may be drumming or dancing in the hope of gaining a few escudos from visitors, and walk by the harbour. Consider having a fish lunch here.
Leaving town, follow the road inland signposted 'Buracona 6km' past stacked containers and warehouses. Soon you'll see West African traders selling curios by the roadside. Behind them lies Regona.

5 Regona

At Regona, inlets of luminous, jewel-like turquoise water are framed by black lava rock. The labyrinths of caverns and horseshoe-shaped tunnels emerging into the open sea are a favourite diving site.
Continue on the Buracona road.

6 Buracona

Monte Leste, rising 263m (863ft) out of the flat stony ground, is literally the high point of this rocky desert area. All the tour groups descend on Buracona (Big Hole) where white-frothed waves crash over black lava rock. There are intriguing light effects in the cavernous 'blue eye'. Clamber across the lava down to a natural swimming pool that fills with calm water while the surf fumes at its rocky edges.
Follow well-worn gravel tracks inland, keeping Monte Leste on your left. Stop before you reach Espargos and look back to see the Terra Boa mirage that shimmers like a sea across the flat plains.

7 Espargos

A scattering of acacia trees, rubbish tips and informal settlements indicate the way into Sal's biggest town. The Esplanada Bom Dia, opposite the Atlantic Hotel, is a popular café with umbrella-shaded tables, but the little Sabura bakery close by has delicious pastries. Next door to Sabura, Art Loja Cabo Verde is a good place to buy island crafts and Cape Verde liqueurs (with tastings).
Leave town on the asphalt road signposted for Pedra de Lume.

8 Pedra de Lume

Stretching out across the crater of a collapsed and long extinct volcano, the Pedra de Lume *salinas* (salt flats) are an intriguing sight. You can float in one of the areas, and check out the healing properties of volcanic mud in another. Showers and changing rooms are available on site.
Return to Espargos and continue south on the wide asphalt road back to Santa Maria.

Salt, the islands' gold

The discovery of vast amounts of salt on Sal, Boavista and Maio was treasure indeed. For nearly four centuries it brought riches to many and was exported all over the world.

In 1578, Sir Francis Drake reported seeing 'huge heaps of salt like drifts of snow' on Maio and it was the English, rather than the colonising Portuguese, who commandeered its extraction. They established a town, Porto Inglês (English Harbour, now Vila do Maio) and thousands of slaves worked to extract the salt from the pans covering the little island.

Shovelled into sacks, the salt was carried by donkeys to the beach. There it was loaded onto boats capable of riding rough seas and heavy swells and would make its way to the English ships lying at anchor off the coast. With about 200 tonnes of the valuable cargo on board, the ships sailed for Newfoundland to pick up cod, salt it and return across the Atlantic to Europe.

Pulleys at the Pedra de Lume salt pans

Up to 11,000 tonnes of salt was exported annually from Maio. Throughout the 17th and 18th centuries the island received an average of 80 English ships a year, all there for the salt that was transported to Europe, Africa, America, the West Indies and, in the 19th century, to Brazil.

It was English sailors who discovered that Boavista, too, had quality salt. There, amid the unforgiving, volcanic red rock landscape they established a settlement. The harbour the English built to export their lucrative find, again named Porto Inglês, is now called Sal Rei (King of Salt). Today the old salt pans outside the town have disappeared, covered by the ever-encroaching sand.

Sal owes its identity to Manuel António Martins, a Cape Verdean trader who had established his flourishing salt business in Boavista at

Pyramids of salt at the disused pans on the outskirts of Santa Maria village

the end of the 18th century. Looking to expand, he moved on to Sal, then known as Llana (Flat Island), and with several hundred slaves began exploiting the rich salt beds that lay in the sunken crater of a long extinct volcano at Pedra de Lume (Stone of Fire).

Martins began exporting from Sal in 1804. Laden donkeys climbed the steep sides of the crater before descending to the harbour with their loads, until a tunnel was made through the rock, dug by hand over several months by the hard labour of slaves. In 1919 a French company took over and installed a cable tramway, enabling the movement of 25 tonnes of salt an hour, which was exported to West and Central Africa.

At Santa Maria, sea water was channelled inland then pumped by wooden windmills into rows of shallow pans. When the water evaporated, the sheets of crystal salt were dug into pyramids. If you brave the outskirts of Santa Maria village today, you'll see the pans and some pyramids. There are replicas of the windmills in town. Carts pulled by mules transported the salt to a newly created harbour, from where 30,000 tonnes a year were exported, mainly to Brazil and later to the Belgian Congo.

A combination of world events eventually saw an end to the salt trade that had brought relative prosperity to three of Cape Verde's islands; Boa Vista's trade ended first in the mid-19th century, Maio's production stopped towards the end of the 19th century while the Sal saltflats fell into disuse in the early 1980s. Now the Cape Verdeans hope tourism will become the new 'gold'.

Boavista

The closest island to the African coast, Boavista has the longest and arguably the most beautiful beaches of all. Like its neighbour Sal, 50km (31 miles) to the north, Boavista is a salt island and, while it isn't as flat as Sal, its hills are no higher than Pico d'Estância at 390m (1,280ft). With a maximum 31km (19 miles) north to south and 29km (18 miles) west to east, it is ringed by 55km (34 miles) of fine-sanded beaches washed by a turquoise blue sea.

Boavista is the third largest island in the Cape Verde archipelago but, with fewer than 5,000 residents, it is the least populated because of an arid landscape and years of droughts that resulted in emigration. This is beginning to change as a building boom attracts workers from other islands. The new international airport, the construction of a massive hotel complex and numerous property developments are all geared to make it a holiday destination for European sun, sea and sand enthusiasts.

The interior of the island is barren, its rust-red colour due to the iron-rich rock, with Saharan dunes shifting in the wind. While brave attempts at agriculture are made in the north, fishing and, increasingly, tourism are the main sources of income for the islanders, most of whom live around the main town, Sal Rei, and in Rabil near the airport. Several villages have been abandoned to the encroaching sand, but those remaining are sleepily attractive, their few streets lined with colourful houses.

Boavista's landscape is extraordinary. There are wide plains of stony red rock, so flat that the hills they reach towards appear positively mountainous, and high desert dunes marching inexorably towards distant habitation. Stands of dusty palm trees form oases in a barren terrain, flat-topped acacia trees provide shade for goats grazing on spiky grass, and tiny lizards are the colour of the sandy ground they dart across. In sight of the ocean, hardy plants bind sand whipped by the wind into undulations, like waves in a gritty white sea. Rough-textured and untamed, this is a world where myriad shades of brown, red, orange and pink are spattered with green and striped by pale sand.

On the northern coast, long, white-capped waves lap beaches furrowed by low dunes. Turtles come ashore to lay their eggs on the sandy shore of a bay to the east. The southern coast has a string of impossibly beautiful beaches that stretch for mile after deserted mile. To the west, watched over by high dunes, 12-km (7½-mile) long Chaves beach captivates all who stay in the hotels and resort developments that line it.

Boavista's story

The idyllic beaches that attract visitors to Boavista today once lured sailors to a sad end, for hidden below the blue waters lie jagged reefs of ferrous rock with a strong magnetic field that play havoc with ships' compasses. The wrecks of over 40 ships lie on the ocean floor, most of them still unexplored.

It is said that the exultant shout of 'Boavista' ('Beautiful sight') by navigators on finally sighting land after long and rough Atlantic sailings led to a change of name for the island that was originally called São Cristóvão when it was discovered on 14 May 1460. When

Boavista

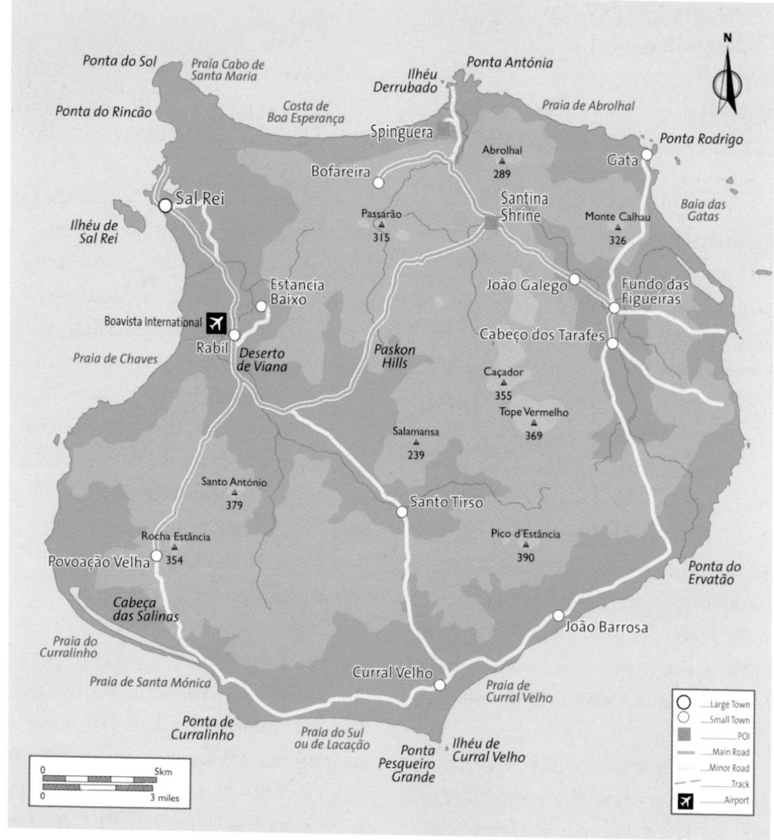

An oasis in the Viana desert

Christopher Columbus landed in 1498, he found lepers among the tiny population and quickly sailed on.

For the following two centuries, the barren landscape seems to have been left mainly to goats, which the early settlers farmed to provide meat and skins for trading with passing ships. A use was found for the island when English sailors discovered good-quality salt there, a valuable commodity in 1620. A settlement grew up inland at Estância (now Povoação Velha) and later at the coast, where the town was named Porto Inglês ('English Harbour', now Sal Rei, 'King of Salt').

The production of salt brought the island prosperity until well into the 19th century. The port's value declined when the deep harbour at Mindelo on São Vicente was created. When the trade in salt died away, island life slipped into abject poverty until the production of lime and clay tiles brought some income in the early 20th century. Old lime kilns, circular drystone structures on the slopes of rocky hills, still dot the landscape. The salt pans have disappeared under sand. Now tourism has the potential to lift Boavista's fortunes and the island's population is increasing.

Sal Rei

One of Sal Rei's main streets is called Rua dos Emigrantes, which reflects the Boavista story. It runs down one side of Largo de Santa Isabel, the main square – which is actually a rectangle – at the heart of the town. Named after the island's patron saint, the square has been planted with trees and shrubs and even has a café and souvenir kiosk. It is edged by low, Portuguese-style architecture and the welcoming church. Churches on most of Cape Verde's islands tend to be kept resolutely shut except for the weekly services, but there are exceptions on Boavista.

Cobbled streets off the big square lead down to the sea, where fishing boats pull up on Praia Diante, the town beach, and children play in the sand and splash through the waves. Women crowd the boats to bargain for the best of the catch and sell their trophies from plastic bowls on the tree-shaded wall nearby. The beachfront road is aptly named Avenida dos Pescadores (Fishermen's Avenue). It's also the site of the tank where water from the town's desalination plant is sold.

HOME OF *MORNA*

Boavista is considered the birthplace of *morna*, the haunting melodies most associated with Cape Verdean music. Its origins are obscure. One theory is that the sounds and repetitive beat are those of fishermen rowing and marking time as they dipped their oars into the sea. Another is that its name derives from the English word 'mourn' and the rhythms are a mix of old Portuguese and Brazilian songs with religious chants, producing a melancholic air that reflects the sadness of slaves longing for their homeland. Boavista's long tradition of *morna* is celebrated with a summer festival held on Sal Rei's town beach.

Dreamcatchers hanging in a Sal Rei window

The church of São Roque in Rabil

Running water is in short supply in the traditional old houses of Sal Rei.

The remains of the Duque de Bragança fort are just visible on an islet across the bay. Boavista was frequently attacked and ransacked by pirates in the 17th and 18th centuries. After a particularly disastrous assault in 1818, the fortress was built as protection for Sal Rei (then known as Porto Inglês), which then prospered.

Going inland, streets narrow, the buildings are colourfully painted, and a range of restaurants and small shops appears on tree-fringed cobbled squares. With a rash of new holiday and second-home apartments on the outskirts, Sal Rei, Boavista's only town, has brightened up considerably. New restaurants have opened, run by their enthusiastic Italian and French owners, and there's a scattering of shops selling crafts, jewellery and souvenirs to tempt visitors.

On Tortuga beach, over the dunes to the south of town, a couple of restaurants with bars hire out sun beds and umbrellas and offer the opportunity for kite surfing or windsurfing.

Rabil

An extended village near the airport, Rabil was once the island's main town. The blue-and-white church of São Roque has an impressive façade and dates from 1801. Below the village to the east, there's an oasis-like canyon with date palms rising from the sand.

THE BEN'OLIEL GRAVES

Near the Marine Club resort outside Sal Rei, a tiny Jewish cemetery sits isolated between the beach and property developments. Encompassed by low stone walls are the graves of the Ben'Oliel family who fled Rabat in 1860 during the persecution of Jews in Morocco, and set up a successful business on Boavista.

The tomb of a young English woman, Julia Maria Pettingall, daughter of one of the administrators of the Luso-British Commission on slavery, lies alongside them. The family left Boavista when yellow fever swept the island, returning when they believed the threat to be over. But sadly it wasn't, and Julia died at the age of 19 in November 1845.

Praia de Chaves (Chaves beach)

This wide, quite spectacular beach of powder-soft white sand stretches for 12km (7½ miles) along the west coast. You can walk there from Sal Rei, 9km (5½ miles) away, crossing Estoril beach along the way, or better still, stay right on the beach at the Parque das Dunas Village hotel (*see p151*) where you go to sleep to the sound of the waves and wake up to a beautiful view.

Nearby there's the strange sight of a tall chimney rising out of the dunes among a group of palm trees – the remains of a former brick factory, abandoned to the sand.

The glorious colours of the sea make this beach look very tempting for swimming, but the waves can be extremely powerful so it's important to check conditions before rushing in.

Povoação Velha

Two wide cobbled streets lined with neat houses make up this sleepy village

Beautiful Chaves beach, on the west coast of Boavista

A colourful bar in Cabeço dos Tarafes

that was the first settlement on the island back in the 17th century. The little white church of St Anthony sits alone on the slope of a rocky hill. Towering above the village at 354m (1,160ft), Rocha Estância is riddled with caves where the people of Povoação Velha sheltered in the days of pirate raids. Unless you plan to climb on the Rocha, the main reason for visiting this village is as a stop along the route to Santa Mónica beach, 6km (4 miles) away.

Praia de Santa Mónica (Santa Mónica beach)

Reached by a steep and winding cobbled road, then a rough track, Santa Mónica beach stretches as far as the eye can see. The most accessible of a line of endless beaches extending along the entire south coast, it has no facilities, so bring everything you need, especially sunblock, shade and plenty of bottled water.

Strong winds and a powerful current drew sailing ships to founder on the reef out to sea, and this beach can be very windblown, especially in the winter months when the Harmattan blows from the Sahara, depositing the sand that has formed the dunes inland.

The three villages

Tucked away in the northeast of the island, João Galego, Fundo das Figueiras and Cabeço dos Tarafes are three villages of brightly coloured houses, their squares and streets lined with blazing red hibiscus bushes and bougainvillea of brilliant hue. This is the 'green' part of Boavista and is full of surprises.

Around the villages, areas of barren ground have been fenced off with dried palm fronds to create fields. Water is siphoned up from deep holes dug in what appears to be a dry riverbed and is used to irrigate the plants. The sight of these patches of green, where onions, tomatoes, melons, potatoes, cabbages and beans thrive, is a welcome one.

If you want a feeling for Boavista's extraordinary landscape, a day's excursion to the villages of the Norte is recommended (*see pp48–9*). The name 'North' harks back to the days when slaves extracting salt around Povoação Velha 'ran north' inland to freedom.

However, unless you have experience driving a four-wheel drive on rough terrain, it's best to hire a vehicle with a driver.

Cabo de Santa Maria

On the north of the island, named after the *Santa Maria*, a Spanish cargo ship that ran aground in 1968, the bay and its extensive, isolated beach is reached over some tough terrain that requires a four-wheel drive vehicle, which you can hire, preferably with a driver.

The ship's rusting hulk lies in the water close to shore, watched over by dunes and ever-shifting sands. You can go for long walks on the dune-furrowed beach and seek out the remains of a petrified forest under a low, eroded cliff, but swimming is not advisable. Not only does the sea tend to be rough, there are sharks out there. The bay looks wildly beautiful, with its turquoise sea and layers of long, white-crested waves reaching for the shore, and fish eagles soar overhead.

To get there, take the 'Pittoresque Route' (a bit of a misnomer) out of Rabil, through struggling date palms and an acacia plantation. The cobbled road, created long ago from stones hand cut by men and laid by women, is in a poor state of repair. At the sign 'Boa Esperança' (Good Hope) turn onto the sand track that meanders through acacia trees and continues for several kilometres across stony ground, bare rock and sand to reach the sea and the wreck of the *Santa Maria*.

One of the pretty houses in Fundo das Figueiras

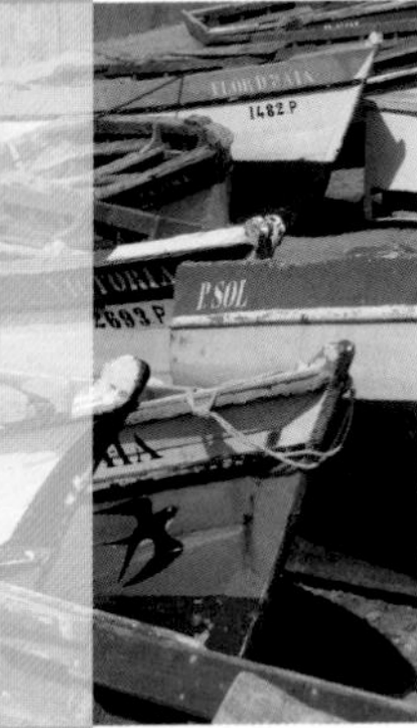

Drive: Highlights of Boavista

An all-terrain vehicle is essential for this route, which offers an overview of Boavista's strange but fascinating landscape and visits three little villages where exotic flowers bloom and colourfully painted houses line the streets. From bare, barren rock to small fields bright with green vegetables, shifting desert dunes and oases of palm trees, the experience will be memorable.

Allow a day for the 60km (37-mile) trip.

Start on the main airport road to Rabil.

1 Rabil

From the main airport road, turn into Rabil. Home to many of the people who work in Sal Rei, it has a few small shops and bars.

Drive through the ribeira *(valley) of struggling date palms and turn onto the road signed 'Deserto de Viana'.*

2 Deserto de Viana (Viana Desert)

Over millennia, wind from the Sahara has deposited sand on Boavista that has drifted into miles of dunes at this point on the island. From a distance the dunes look like a pale sea sandwiched between pink-red hills. Up close, their sinuous lines intrigue.

On the right as you wind back towards the Rabil road, there's a steep stony hill topped by an abandoned church. Climb it for panoramic views over the dunes and across to the village of Estância de Baixo. At the Rabil road junction, take the left fork marked 'Norte'.

3 Over the Paskon Hills

The cobbled road cuts straight through a flat, bare, rock desert landscape where goats feed on scrub plants, crossing dry riverbeds that flood when the rains come and turn the area green. Over the stone-quarried Paskon Hills, look for screened-off areas where vegetables are grown using drip irrigation.

*A wayside shrine at Santina marks the turn off left to Spinguera, an Italian-designed eco-hotel (*see p151*) by Espingueira village, and the isolated village of Bofareira. (The track to Spinguera passes a low canyon, its sides eroded into contorted shapes.) Continue on the Norte road towards João Galego.*

4 João Galego

Approaching the village, you'll see areas of cultivation in arid surroundings, particularly in the late summer and early winter months when an amazing array of vegetables are grown.

Stroll through the three, tree-lined cobbled streets, passing houses painted

in bright colours with bougainvillea clambering over porches. A scattering of hens peck for crumbs among the hibiscus bushes, sleepy dogs raise an eye, and giggling children play. João Galego is home to about 600 people.
The road continues on to the next village, Fundo das Figueiras, a short distance away.

5 Fundo das Figueiras

Even more colourful, and seemingly the most prosperous of the three villages (*see pp46–7*), Fundo das Figueiras has more of those brightly painted houses with their contrasting shutters, the town square is packed with red hibiscus flowers, and the gleaming white Church of St John the Baptist is lovingly cared for.

First, call in to see Bia at the spotless little Restaurante Nha Terra and ask what she can offer for lunch, and then wander round the village while she cooks it. The population of 400 is well catered for here, with a post office, kindergarten, primary school, youth centre, football pitch and games ground.
Continue on the road out of the village.

6 Cabeço dos Tarafes

With only 200 inhabitants, this is the smallest of the villages. The school has been turned into a social centre and the children travel to nearby Fundo das Figueiras for lessons.
Return along the road back to Rabil and Sal Rei.

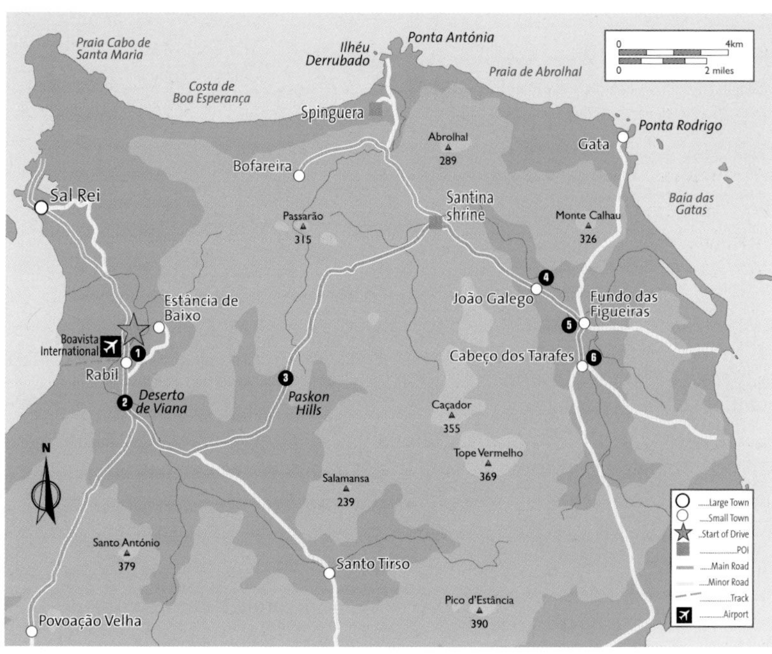

Shipwrecks off Cape Verde's coast

Treacherous reefs off the islands' coasts have caused the demise of hundreds of sailing ships. The most notorious reef was that of Boavista, where a combination of strong trade winds, a powerful current dragging ships to the shore, the red rock with its iron content that sent compasses awry, inaccurate charts, and at certain times of the year the sand-laden Harmattan from the Sahara blowing over the island and covering it in a misty haze, all combined to lure ships to their doom. Captain Cook narrowly avoided disaster there in 1776.

A 6-km (4-mile) long reef off Boavista's northeastern coast bears the name Hartwell Reef after a ship that sank there in 1787. A British East India Company ship, the *Hartwell* sailed from Britain in February 1787 on her maiden voyage to China, bearing an extremely rich cargo that included 5.9 million grams (209,280oz) of fine silver. Gales put her badly behind schedule and she'd been at sea almost three months when a mutiny broke out on board. The captain, who was the brother of the ship's owner, John Fiott, set a change of course to put the mutineers ashore and into the charge of the Governor of Cape Verde, only to come to grief off Boavista. The crew were saved but the cargo was lost.

A wreck lying off the Boavista coast

The *Princess Louisa* was ten years old and on what was planned to be her fourth and last long voyage when she ran aground and broke in two on the Baixo de Galeão reef off Maio on 18 April 1743. A three-masted, two-deck ship, mounted with 30 guns, she was named after King George II's youngest daughter, who became the Queen of Denmark in the very year the ship sank. *Princess Louisa* was bound for Persia and India and carried a cargo that included 20 chests of Spanish silver coins, gunpowder, woollen textiles, iron guns and 820 elephant tusks. The ship's surgeon,

Artefacts salvaged from wrecks on display in the Praia Shipwreck Museum

who survived the ordeal in the shark-infested sea only to be robbed of his diamond ring when he struggled ashore naked, reported that the men had 'drunk themselves into oblivion to ease their passage into the next world'. There were 41 survivors but 74 men died that night. The ship's wreck was found and excavated in 1998.

A French East India ship, *Dromodaire*, had 154 people on board when she sailed for India in 1762 carrying 20 guns and 2,000 cannon balls in expectation of trouble. Appalling weather conditions off Cape Verde made navigational instruments useless, so the ship's position could only be estimated; so close to land on São Vicente did *Dromodaire* come that the breakers could be heard. She was soon carried by the current onto a treacherous reef, where she broke in two. In a state of panic, the crew did not follow orders and half of their number perished.

For the poverty-ridden and drought-stricken islanders, salvage from a shipwreck could mean survival, and there are stories of ships being lured to shore with lights. Many of the timbers and fittings of a Dutch ship that sank off Maio in 1781 were sold to the Bishop of Cape Verde for the construction of a new church.

To see some of the fascinating discoveries made from these ships and others, visit the Shipwreck Museum in Praia (*see p80*).

São Vicente

Island of musicians, poets, artists and craftspeople, São Vicente is the cultural heart of Cape Verde. One of the Barlavento (Windward) group, the big attraction is its main town, Mindelo, which curves around a deep harbour in the shadow of 774m (2,540ft) high Monte Verde. A small, red-rock arid island about 16km (10 miles) at its longest and 24km (15 miles) at its widest, most of its 70,000 inhabitants live in and around Mindelo.

This is the home of Cesária Évora, Cape Verde's world-famous exponent of *morna* music, and it is music that attracts many visitors to São Vicente. It drifts from open windows and lively bars, while some of the country's best musicians play in restaurants and in the clubs that make Mindelo the capital of Cape Verdean nightlife. The island hosts a renowned international music

São Vicente (*see pp60–61 for orange route drive*)

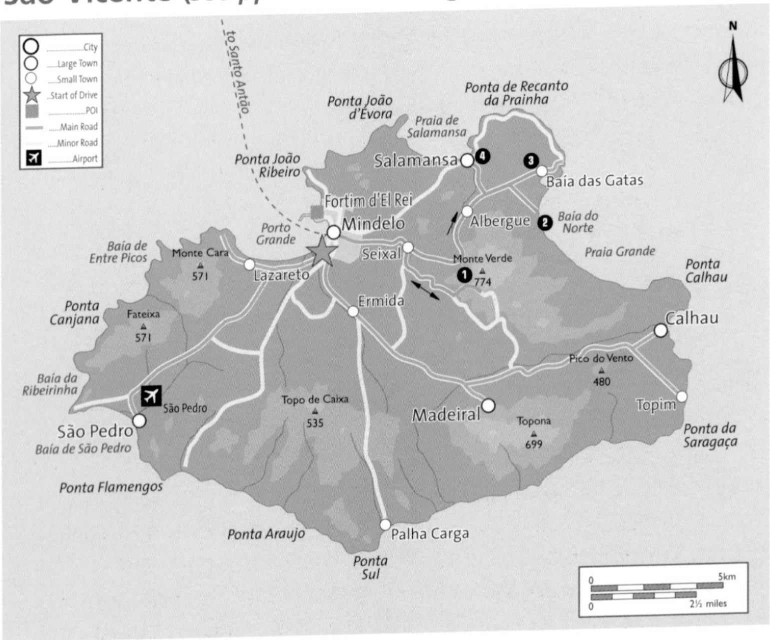

Mindelo harbour with Monte Verde in the background

festival on the beach in August and a theatre festival in September, Mindelact, that's considered West Africa's best, but it is most famous for its Carnival. Events, parades and partying begin over the weekend before Ash Wednesday. With their vibrant colour, fantastic floats, dazzling costumes and pulsating music, the parades rival those of Brazil. At the heart of the five-day extravaganza, the spectacular *Escola de Samba Tropical* parade winds through Mindelo's main streets, cheered on by thousands of enthusiastic spectators and followed by the all-night partying that's an essential ingredient of Cape Verdean Carnival.

The island was discovered on 22 January 1492, St Vincent's day, hence its name, but due to its barren interior and complete lack of water, São Vicente only came to life in the 19th century. This was when Mindelo Bay, which fills the collapsed crater of an ancient volcano, attracted British interest as a deepwater harbour in which to establish a coaling station to re-supply transatlantic shipping. British, Portuguese and Brazilian influences give Mindelo, Cape Verde's second largest city, a distinctly European air.

Mindelo

Tree-lined streets, cobbled squares and brightly coloured colonial buildings distinguish Mindelo's town centre. A mix of British and Portuguese architecture lines the wide streets that have a varied collection of restaurants, bars, cafés and shops. You can spot the British-built houses by their sloping tiled roofs.

With islands of palm trees down its centre, traffic-busy Avenida da

One of Mindelo's tree-lined streets

República (Avenida Marginal, north of the old Customs House) sweeps the length of the harbour. The best views of Mindelo are from the Santo Antão ferry terminal at the port. From here you can see how the town lines the curving bay at the foot of Monte Verde and shelters in the arms of high hills.

Another good viewpoint is **Fortim d'El Rei**, on the headland to the east. The ruined fort and former prison seems destined to be the site of a tourist resort and casino. The view encompasses Monte Cara (Face Mountain) across the magnificent boat-dotted Porto Grande harbour, the strange stack of Ilhéu dos Pássaros (Bird Island) rising from the sea, and the outline of Santo Antão on the horizon. Looking inland you get a good perspective on Mindelo, the old town and its new suburbs clambering into the foothills.

Mindelo's favourite meeting place is the Praça Nova (officially renamed Praça Amílcar Cabral, its old name is in general use), a long square filled with shady trees and flowering shrubs. At 10pm the Praça is the scene of an evening stroll that is Mindelo's version of the Italian *passeggiata*. Here it is known as the *trapiche* after the circular motion of the old sugar-cane presses used in the making of *grogue* (the local alcoholic drink). At the top of the square, a brightly painted, very British bandstand is still in use. It's a long-held local tradition to bring children to hear the brass band play on Sunday, 'family day', around 7pm.

The lively indoor **Mercado Municipal** (Municipal Market) is on wide Rua Lisboa. Much of the produce comes from neighbouring Santo Antão, less than an hour away by ferry. São Vicente receives very little rain and virtually nothing grows on its scorched, dusty and rocky soil. The busy fish market down by the port, however, is testament to the fruits of the sea. There are small shops on the upper floor of the Mercado Municipal building.

Blue and white tiles painted with scenes from Mindelo's busy past as a refuelling station for ships decorate the general market, where West African traders sell clothing and household goods.

There have been bag-snatchings and the occasional robbery of tourists in Mindelo, so keep an eye on valuables. It's one of the few places in Cape Verde where you may be approached by beggars, not all of them genuine. If you are going out at night, especially clubbing, it's advisable to take a taxi even a short distance.

For a walk through town, see pp58–9.

CHINESE *LOJAS*

The arrival of Chinese-run shops in the mid 1990s changed the lives of most islanders. Selling an array of goods imported from China, but particularly affordable clothing, they put an end to children going barefoot and gave parents the possibility of buying toys at Christmas. Each town has its Chinese *lojas*, which sell everything from household goods to cosmetics and schoolbooks. As one Mindelo woman explained, 'We had so little money, and the *lojas* brought dignity, self-esteem and a quality of life to the people of Cape Verde.'

The British influence in Mindelo

In 1838, Lieutenant John Lewis of the British East India Company secured a

British-style houses in Mindelo

licence for a floating coal bunker on São Vicente and brought coal from Cardiff to stock it. By 1860, six British coal companies had the monopoly on the trading of coal and the refuelling of ships en route for the Americas and the Cape of Good Hope. In 1889, about 2,000 merchant vessels were anchored in Mindelo Bay. With the laying of a submarine cable for transatlantic communication in 1874, employees of Western Telegraph added to the British contingent.

A sports club was formed in 1879; a cricket club in 1918. The (very brown and dusty) golf course is still in use. On Municipality Day, 22 January, the British joined in the festivities by running races and singing 'It's a Long Way to Tipperary' and 'For He's a Jolly

The view over São Pedro Bay

ENGLISH WORDS

The British presence in Mindelo left a legacy of English words and expressions that became incorporated into Crioulo. Among them are *bois* (boys), *xuinigom* (chewing gum), *speed fast* (full speed), *ariope* (hurry up), *ovatime* (overtime), *chatope* (shut up), *blaqafela* (black fellow), *salonge* (so long) and *bossomane* (boss man). If a person you know passes by without a greeting, he is said to go *strate* (straight by).

Jintonc (gin and tonic) is still favoured as the pre-lunch drink in Mindelo bars. The names of the national drinks *grogue* and *ponche* (*grogue* sweetened with cane syrup) are derived from the English words 'grog' and 'punch'.

Good Fellow'. At Christmas, people lining up in front of the Western Telegraph building were given cinema tickets bearing a picture of John Bull and his bulldog.

São Pedro

Mountain-backed Baía de São Pedro (São Pedro Bay) lies a short distance from the airport, about 10km (6 miles) from the centre of Mindelo. It's a big hit with windsurfers, but the waves and a strong current make it unsafe for swimming. Bright fishing boats pull up on the sand at one end of the beach. They are watched over by a cluster of little stone-built houses, home to a fishing community whose water supply is trucked in daily from the island's desalination plant. The water collection point is at the entrance to the village. In revealing contrast, right next to it there's a Cape Verde Telecom mast to boost mobile phone reception in this hilly region.

Baía das Gatas (Catfish Bay)

East of Mindelo, 12km (7½ miles) away via a well-kept cobbled road, Baía das Gatas has a growing collection of smart holiday and second homes that makes it lively at weekends but somewhat bleak during the week. A reef forming a natural lagoon means it is the best place for swimming on São Vicente, and anglers find easy catches among the rocks.

In August, the Baía das Gatas Music Festival attracts huge crowds for sporting events, horse racing and a huge selection of music, with local and international groups and solo artists performing (*see p21*).

The area is destined for great change, with huge property developments that include hotels, villas, apartments and Ernie Els-designed golf courses.

SANTA LUZIA

Off the southeast coast of São Vicente, Santa Luzia is Cape Verde's only uninhabited island. During the 19th century, a small community settled there to breed goats, to fish, and to extract a dye from earth orchid lichen for export to West Africa. Just 13km (8 miles) long and 5km (3 miles) wide, it has no fresh water and vegetation is scarce. There are beaches and dunes in the south, and steep slopes in the north. Fishermen from Calhau often sail out here, and you can negotiate with them for the two-hour trip. Sometimes group tours are available; check with a travel agent in Mindelo.

Walk: Mindelo town

Mindelo's history comes to life as you stroll the wide, tree-lined streets.

Allow two or three unhurried hours for the 3-km (2-mile) walk and enjoy the atmosphere.

Start at the Praça Nova, everyone's favourite square.

1 Praça Nova (New Square)

High walls enclosed this leafy, flower-filled park when the British created it in 1891, and only British and Portuguese residents were allowed in.

Cross Rua Patrice Lumumba, walking south by the blue-shuttered Cape Verde Telecom building that occupies the site of Mindelo's first (British-built) hospital into Avenida 5 de Julho.

2 Avenida 5 de Julho

Mindelo's oldest street was almost entirely a British preserve. On the left, next to the Kathedral Bar (a former chapel), look for the pretty little house hidden behind a shady almond tree. Dating from 1850, it was the Deposit Office of coal company Miller and Cory. On the right, next to Club Nautico, the pink-painted building is the old Customs House.

Turn right into Rua Lisboa. Passing the pretty blue-and-white Alliance Française building at the end, turn left into Avenida da República.

3 Torre de Belem (Belem Tower)

The Avenida da República follows the deep harbour bay. An eagle monument commemorates Portuguese aviators Sacadura Cabral and Gago Coutinho, who landed on São Vicente in 1922 before completing the first flight across the South Atlantic. Further along, fishermen sit under the shade of trees beside a statue of Diogo Afonso, the Portuguese navigator who discovered the island. The Torre de Belem used to be the harbour master's office. Check out the activity in the nearby fish market.

Most of the buildings on the left as you walk along the Avenida were the homes of British people working for the coaling station companies and also for the Western Telegraph. A submarine cable for transatlantic communication was laid in the late 19th century and the company employed many British people. Look for the striking Poema Mindelense mural.

Go left past the fish market to Praça Estrela and market stalls, where images of old Mindelo are painted on tiles. Cross Rua Eduardo de Baisemão and turn left into Rua da Luz.

4 Pracinha da Igreja (Church Square)

In one of the earliest residential areas, cobbled Rua da Luz, with its pastel-painted houses, leads to this attractive square and the Catholic church built in 1862. Beyond, stands the impressive Câmara Municipal (Town Hall). Explore the stalls of fruit, vegetables and medicinal herbs in the Mercado Municipal, then stop at tiny Café Lisboa, a favourite meeting place for Mindelo's intellectuals, or look for the entrance to Nella's, one of Mindelo's most atmospheric restaurants, on the left as you pass the market. Turn right into Rua Lisboa. The splendid pink Palácio do Povo ('People's Palace', the President's palace), unfortunately not open to the public, stands at the top of the street. *Turn left at the top by the Palaçio into Avenida Baltazar Lopes da Silva.*

5 Avenida Baltazar Lopes da Silva

Trees shade this wide street lined with boutiques, shops, offices, apartments and colonial architecture. Go left into Rua Patrice Lumumba, taking a look at the little British-built houses, in need of renovation, that line narrow Rua António Aurelio da Silva Gonçalves on your left. Now you are back at the Praça Nova, but don't miss the Arte Crioula shop on the corner. It's the best place in Cape Verde to buy crafts (*see p126*).

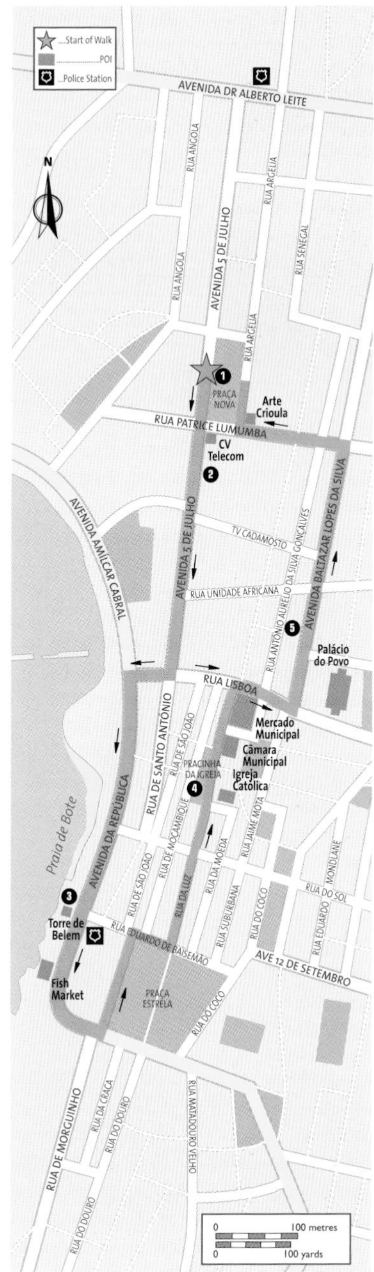

Drive: São Vicente, beach and mountain

Combine sea, sand and panoramic views on this drive across the top of the island. If you do this in the afternoon and it's a clear day, head first for the beach and later watch the sun set across the bay from the top of Monte Verde.

See map on page 52 for route.

The drive is 42km (26 miles) and will take half a day.

Leave Mindelo on Avenida 12 de Setembro. At the roundabout by the Shell petrol station, take the road signposted Baía das Gatas/Monte Verde.

1 Monte Verde

Leaving Mindelo behind, you begin to see why the colonial British called arid, red-rock São Vicente 'the cinder heap'. After about 7km (4½ miles), take the right turn marked 'Monte Verde'. The cobbled road zigzagging up the mountainside passes between neatly terraced fields crying out for rain. Stop and admire the panoramic view from the top, which encompasses

The road up to Monte Verde passes arid slopes and brave attempts at terraced fields

The modern church at Salamansa on a ridge above the sea

craggy mountains and an island-dotted sea.

Return down the mountain to meet the road marked 'Baía das Gatas'.

2 Baía do Norte (North Bay)

The Baía das Gatas road meanders down through high hills of red rock. Turn right at the 'Norte Baía' sign onto an asphalt road to see Saharan sand contrasting with black, red and grey volcanic rock. Beyond the dunes lies white-sanded Praia Grande beach on Baía do Norte, with Pico do Vento volcano (480m/1,575ft) in the background. A resort complex is being built here.

Return to the cobbled road, turning right for Baía das Gatas.

3 Baía das Gatas (Catfish Bay)

Weekends are the best time to see 'Catfish Bay' in action, though this may change as the hotels, resorts and property developments come to fruition. The beach is sandy and you can swim in the natural lagoon.

The horizon seems to be hung with mountains as you drive back towards Mindelo. Take a signposted right fork to Salamansa.

4 Salamansa

This hillside fishing village has a school, a shop, a football club, some big houses and a fabulous sea view from the church.

Go back to the main road and turn right to return to Mindelo.

Sounds of the Cape Verdean soul

Music is the lifeblood of Cape Verde. The African drumming of *batuque*, the lively beat of *funaná* and the longing of the *morna* all brought colour into the lives of a people living in harsh and extreme conditions, providing a welcome break from their daily struggles for survival. Today, while reggae and zouk are popular with young Cape Verdeans, traditional music still plays an important role in everyday life and is an integral part of festivals and social gatherings. You'll hear it on the streets and in restaurants and bars.

Dancing to *funaná* on Sal

Performed by village women on Santiago, usually at celebrations such as weddings and festivals, *batuque* is the oldest form of music on the islands. African slaves, unable to find the tree trunks and animal hides needed to make their traditional drums (or forbidden to do so by their owners), improvised by using the *pano* cotton they wove into patterned scarves and shawls. They placed the material, tightly rolled into drum-like balls, between their knees and pounded it with the palms of their hands.

Sitting in a semi-circle, singers start the chant known as *finaçon*, changing the pace and mood, maintaining the beat by hitting their palms against their thighs. The song is improvised, a legacy of the African tradition. Accompanied by the beating of pano drums in a complex and multi-layered rhythm, a dancer moves to the centre. She begins slowly, rhythmically and suggestively, increasing in pace to a whirlwind peak of gyrating hips, pounding drums and a crescendo of singing. Then another dancer takes her place.

Funaná also originates from Santiago but from the early 20th

The festival stage by the beach in Baía das Gatas on São Vicente

century. Played on a *gaito*, a type of accordion, and a knife rubbed against a small metal bar (the *ferro*), it has a lively beat with African and Brazilian influences and the dancing is sensuous. It celebrates the joy of living. In recent years, recordings by dance bands using keyboards, guitars and drums have given it a wider audience.

Coladeira, a fast-tempo, late-night dance music incorporating African and Afro-American sounds, emerged from the processional dance performed at festivals on São Vicente and neighbouring Santo Antão.

The *Tabanka* festivals performed by defiant African slaves on Santiago have almost died out now, but the music, performed on conch shell horns, drums and now accordion, is being revived by some Cape Verdean-American groups. The accordion was introduced to the islands by the Catholic Church at the turn of the last century as a portable alternative to the organ.

Thanks to Cesária Évora, known worldwide as the 'barefoot diva', and her trademark song 'Sodade', the most famous of all Cape Verdean music is the *morna*. Ballads expressing the sadness of parting and the longing for return, *mornas* are full of emotion and sung from the heart. They speak of longing and sadness, passion and pain and are the most European of all the Cape Verdean music genres.

Mornas are sung to the accompaniment of traditional stringed instruments, *rabeças* (violins), *violão* (guitars) and *cavaquinhos*, which bear a likeness to the ukulele. You can see the instruments being made by hand at the **Aniceto Gomes Atelier de Violão** in Mindelo, *Monte Sossego, behind the cemetery. Tel: 914 623.*

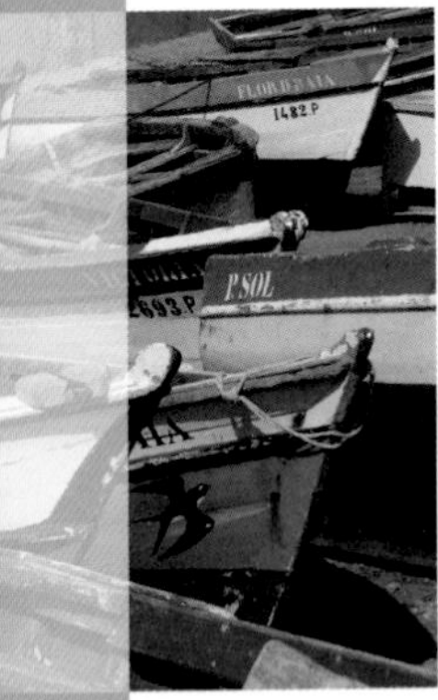

Santo Antão

Islands don't get much more spectacular than Santo Antão. Only a ferry ride away from dry and dusty São Vicente, it feels like another world. At the western end of the Barlavento (Windward) group, it is the most northerly of all the Cape Verde islands and, with a surface area of 779sq km (300sq miles), the second largest. The scattered population of 50,000 lives mainly in the northeast and in the ferry port town of Porto Novo.

High mountains define Santo Antão. A long chain of them stretches from the northeast to the southwest, splitting an island that spans 43km (27 miles) at its longest and 24km (15 miles) at its widest points. Topo de Coroa's volcanic peak is the highest point, reaching 1,979m (6,493ft). The spectacular green

Santo Antão (*see pp72–3 for orange route drive*)

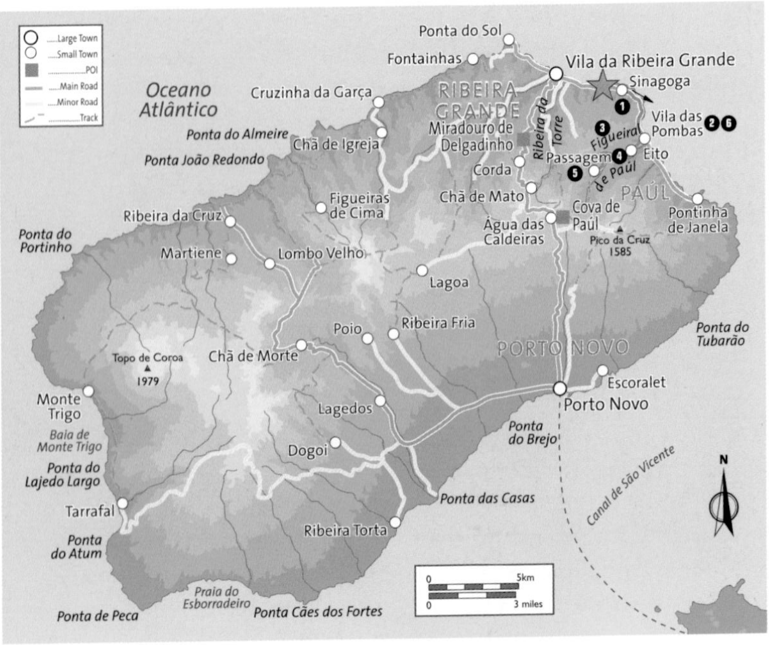

The view of Porto Novo from the ferry

landscapes of the north and east contrast with the barren south and the deep ravines, craters and cliffs that make the west almost inaccessible. This is truly an island of extremes.

Pastel-painted houses lining the red cliffs at Porto Novo present a pretty scene as the ferry approaches the harbour bay. Leaving town, bare brown hills are streaked with creamy *pozzolana*, a volcanic dust that is used in the making of cement and is one of Santo Antão's exports.

The road climbs doggedly upwards, lined by aloe vera with spikes of yellow flowers, planted to bind the dusty red soil at its edges. The fleshy leaves echo the colours of the rocks, while the scorched bare earth yields little but stones. Yet crest the highest hill and you think your eyes must be deceiving you. Welcome to the dramatic beauty of Santo Antão.

Amazing vistas

Over the ridge all is green. High in the pinewoods the air is clear and fresh and everywhere you look there are mountains, layer after rugged layer of them, their folds terraced into tiny, vertiginous fields. Villages hide in lush valleys, tiny settlements cling precariously to ledges on cliffs with dizzying drops.

This is a world of jagged peaks, deep crevices, colossal volcanic walls and jaw-dropping ravines, of nature's sculptures carved by the elements into tortured shapes and sheer rock faces, planted green, plunging dramatically from the roadside.

In an extraordinary feat of human endeavour, the 36km (22-mile) cobbled road, ten years in the making, was dug and created in the 1960s without mechanical assistance, each hand-hewn piece of volcanic stone individually laid. With tight corners and blind bends it twists and turns, following the mountain contours, crossing ridges and circling craters, before ending in the busy little coastal town of Ribeira Grande. This has to count as one of the world's most spectacular drives.

Gloriously green

At high altitudes and often surrounded by clouds, cedar and pine trees, eucalyptus and mimosa thrive in the cool air. Apple orchards cover slopes in the mid regions, fields of sugar cane pack into ravines while bananas and mangoes flourish in humid valleys.

Cova de Paúl, the giant crater of an extinct volcano 305m (1,000ft) deep, is intensively farmed. The soil at its base supports potatoes, beans, maize and good harvests of sweet potatoes for the subsistence farmers who rent the patchwork of small fields. Coffee is grown on the terraced sides.

At Água das Caldeiras, a small pumping station belies its significance. The fresh water pumped from the depths is driven by tanker to be bought and sold in Porto Novo. Before the desalination plant was built in Mindelo, it was shipped across to the residents of São Vicente, Santo Antão's parched neighbour.

The cobbled road across the mountains passes through small villages like Espongeiro, famed for the quality of its goat's cheese, much favoured as a dessert accompanied by papaya or mango preserves. It winds on towards Chã de Mato, on a bend with amazing views down the fertile Ribeira da Torre, and zigzags wildly before reaching Corda, where cloud and humidity play their part in providing moisture for the steeply terraced fields.

Looking down on the fields within the Cova de Paúl crater

A view of Santo Antão's mountains plunging dramatically from the roadside

From Corda, the views are even more spectacular. When the road crosses a narrow ridge between two mountains at the Miradouro de Delgadinho, there are sheer drops on either side. Ribeira da Torre lies far below on the right and Ribeira Grande, with a spattering of perched villages, on the left.

Big spikey aloes frame panoramic vistas of craggy peaked mountain ranges that hang on the horizon and, layer by layer, appear to march towards you. Rain-capturing terraces transform the rock face into fertile fields and tiny plots so steep you wonder how they were ever made, never mind sown and harvested. They look impossible to reach.

The impenetrable landscape made settlement difficult in the early years after the discovery of the island in 1462. The first Portuguese settlers arrived in 1548 and the fertile land of the northeast would eventually provide the richest source of fruit and vegetables in the entire archipelago. The intensity of the cultivation and the variety of the crops are evident as the road winds down to the coast, coming to its end at Vila da Ribeira Grande, squeezed between cliffs and the sea, from where *alugueres* (minibus taxis) leave for

COMPANION PLANTING

Maize and beans are grown together, the maize providing the prop for beans to climb. Although maize requires plenty of water to grow tall, the bean plants can survive with less moisture, so if too little rain falls there's still the possibility of getting at least one vegetable crop.

Santo Antão is an island of subsistence farmers, growing crops for the family's food. In recent years the rains have been sporadic, often arriving at the end of the year instead of July to September as expected. This upsets the planting season and can diminish the quality of the harvest the farmers rely on.

HIKING ON SANTO ANTÃO

Most of the visitors on day excursions from Mindelo wish they'd arranged to stay longer on the island. For keen walkers, hiking in the *ribeiras* (valleys) and mountains is an exhilarating experience. The majority of routes are on cobbled paths used by the local people and can be plotted from a hiking map.

While some of the high mountain routes require determination and some skill, for the inexperienced walker there are easy, fairly flat walks through the lower *ribeiras* that are very scenic and hugely enjoyable.

Ponta do Sol and the villages lining the lushest *ribeiras* (valleys) on the island.

A new coastal road linking Porto Novo with the Santo Antão Resort (a new resort of villas and apartments still under construction), and incorporating Cape Verde's first tunnel, will make the journey from Ribeira Grande to the ferry much easier, if less scenic. It will certainly help with the transport of goods. Incredible as it seems today, before the road was laid across the mountains, the tortuous route to Porto Novo was made by donkey or mule and took days to complete.

Vila da Ribeira Grande

Vila da Ribeira Grande, known locally as Povoação, a bustling town of narrow streets with its shops, schools, churches and hospital, has some colonial Portuguese architecture and a collection of thatched stone houses in the old part of town. It's a good place to stock up on supplies and petrol, but 'sights' are thin on the ground. The main church, **Nossa Senhora do Rosário**, dates from the mid-18th century, a period when Santo Antão might have gained some prominence because the Bishop abandoned unsanitary Santiago and decided to take up residence in Ribeira Grande. However, the See was eventually granted to the island of São Nicolau.

From the *vila* there are scenic coastal drives to Ponta do Sol and hiking in the stunning *ribeiras* of Paúl, Torre and Grande.

Ponta do Sol

Santo Antão's administrative centre is based around a fishing harbour. From the shore, wide streets lined with colour-

A typical cobbled road on Santo Antão

The coastline at Ponta do Sol

washed houses lead up the hill towards the main square, where the elegant mustard-coloured **Câmara Municipal** (Town Hall) and 19th-century church face each other across gardens.

Ponta do Sol has a spaciousness and openness that Ribeira Grande lacks. It is brighter and cleaner, too. There's a modern hotel overlooking the square and the smart blocks of apartments for rent near the harbour have been integrated into the town, rather than standing as separate tourist blocks as often happens on Cape Verde. With the opening of several new restaurants, Ponta do Sol has become a viable place to stay on the island and will doubtless expand.

Santo Antão is relatively undeveloped in terms of tourism, and gleaning local information can prove quite difficult. Good maps with hiking routes are available and can be bought at Cabo Verde Bikes in the main street, which organises tours and treks as well as renting out mountain bikes (*see p155*). It also has a snack bar/pizzeria and sells crafts and locally made jams and liqueurs.

Down at the harbour, colourful fishing boats pull up on the sand and powerful waves pound the rocks and harbour wall. On the drive from Ribeira Grande, the road hugs the coast, and sheer-sided mountains fall straight into the ocean.

A *trapiche* used for making *grogue*, in Paúl

Paúl

The district of Paúl runs back from the coast, where soaring cliffs fall headlong into the pounding surf and lead back to beautifully scenic *ribeiras.* Cut into the mountainside, the road from Vila da Ribeira Grande passes small coastal communities like **Sinagoga**, where exiled Portuguese Jews settled in the 19th century and a leper colony existed on a wave-lashed promontory. Multicoloured layers of rock loom, harsh and forbidding, above the houses.

Vila das Pombas comes into view as you drive around the many bends in the serrated coastline, a splash of colour snuggling under a towering rock face. A collection of brightly painted houses lines the bay, where the beach is gritty volcanic sand and the sea foams white over shiny black rocks. Behind the houses, the narrow streets have more homes and some food shops, several of them doing double duty as bars.

A statue of Santo António watches over the little town from its perch high above on a rocky hill. The climb to it is steep, but there are great views out

THE MAKING OF *GROGUE*

Distilled entirely from sugar cane, *grogue* is a lethally alcoholic spirit that is an essential part of Cape Verdean culture. However, for most of us it is probably best described as an 'acquired taste'.

Traditionally, the sugar cane was pressed through a *trapiche*, a large wooden contraption driven by oxen, which plodded in circles pushing the long pole that worked the creaking machine's heavy metal rollers. It wasn't unusual for men to lose a limb while feeding the cut sugar cane into those rollers, and several sad songs have been written about the working lives of the *grogue* makers.

The extracted juice was collected and left to ferment for a week to ten days. It was then placed in an oven created by piling up stones, and brought to boil over a fire fed by dried sugar-cane leaves. The steam was directed through a pipe cooled with water, and the distilled spirit began to appear.

Much of the *grogue* drunk in villages today is likely to be made in backyard oil drums, so to see a traditional *trapiche* in operation is an opportunity worth taking. Senhor Ildo's 500-year-old *trapiche* in Paúl is one of the few still surviving in Cape Verde and his *grogue* is made in the the traditional way (*see opposite*).

The *grogue*-distilling season runs from January or February to July, depending on the growth of the sugar-cane crop, but even if you visit outside of these months you can see the machine in the yard and taste and buy the brew.

over the ocean and inland across the lush *ribeira*. The saint's feast day is 13 June, a time of great celebration with music, processions and a feast of food and drink.

Along the coast road below the statue there's a battered wooden door set into a long white wall. Go through it, and the pathway will lead you to **Senhor Ildo Benrós Silva's distillery** (*tel: 223 1364*) where *grogue*, Cape Verde's favourite alcoholic drink, is made in the traditional way using an oxen-driven *trapiche*. You'll think you've stepped back into a different century.

Traditional houses in Paúl district

Ribeira do Paúl

Mango, almond and spreading, glossy-leaved breadfruit trees stand tall above the countless fields of sugar cane and bananas that fill Paúl's wide *ribeira*, a valley reminiscent of a lush Caribbean island.

The cobbled road that winds up the valley connects little villages and affords views of hillside farms, their cattle and their houses. Papaya fruits cluster above peanut plants and coffee bushes, while fields of maize and beans vie for space among the potatoes, cabbages and sweet potatoes.

At the entrance to the *ribeira* at **Figueiral de Paúl**, yams are grown in a stream that flows all year. Nearby there's a cluster of small, traditional stone houses, whitewashed and thatched with the leaves of sugar cane plants that have been dried and bound with mountain sisal. The houses have electricity and are home to a community of about 100 people. Further up the valley, **Eito** is a much bigger village of more modern homes, surrounded by fields and huge breadfruit trees. Eito is on the way up to **Passagem**, where paths lead down to a municipal park in the valley. At weekends it's packed with families who come to picnic, walk in the gardens and swim in the pool. Where the road ends, about a 20-minute drive later, zigzagging hiking paths lead up to the rim of the **Cova de Paúl** crater.

Drive: Santo Antão, surf and sugar cane

This 24-km (15-mile) route takes you along a jagged coastline to the lush valley fields of Paúl. It is a pleasant half-day tour, or a full day if you go walking in the valley.

See page 64 for map.

After the Shell garage in Vila da Ribeira Grande, turn right along the coast. The road ascends, hugging the mountainside as long, white-crested waves roll onto black rocks below.

1 Sinagoga

There's just a small community living here now, huddled under the multi-coloured layers of rock that tower above the houses, but in the early 19th century, it was home to exiled Portuguese Jewish families, and a small cemetery still remains. Jews have a long history in Cape Verde and played an important role in the culture and genetic mix of the islands. Most of them fled to escape the Inquisition or were exiled for political reasons. On Santo Antão, those who settled in the mountains became leading traders.

The crumbling building on the peninsula was used to house people with leprosy until well into the 20th century.

Continue south on the coast road to Vila das Pombas.

2 Vila das Pombas

Colourful houses line the seafront, watched over by a statue of St Anthony high on a craggy outcrop. A steep 15-minute climb to the top will reward you with grand views over the coast and inland across the lush, green fertile valleys. The narrow streets of the little town have shops with dark interiors that often double as bars.

Continue along Avenida Januário Leite, turning right after the big rubber tree and crossing the riverbed to meet the road heading inland along the valley.

3 Into the Figueiral de Paúl

Traditional whitewashed stone houses, thatched with dried leaves, huddle by a stream where yams grow in the water. The houses are simple but have electricity and television and, tiny as it may seem, this thriving little community is home to about 100 people. The thatch on the roofs has to be replaced every one to two years and is made by drying and binding reeds

collected from the surrounding area.
Continue along the road towards Eito.

4 Eito

The valley's biggest village straddles both sides of the road and clambers up the hill. The massive breadfruit trees around here are particularly impressive. Among groves of mango and almond trees, the tilled fields are packed with myriad vegetables and the sugar cane grown to make *grogue.*
Continue along the road towards Passagem, passing a small farm in the valley where well-fed cows graze.

5 Passagem

A good place for a picnic, this municipal park at the bottom of a valley is bright with bougainvillea. There's a swimming pool among the trees and well-tended flowery gardens. At weekends, it is a popular spot for local families.
From here you can turn back, or continue up the winding road to its end, about another 20 minutes of driving past villages perched on vertiginous slopes and houses crammed on to ledges, from where a steep uphill hiking path leads into the extinct volcano crater of Cova de Paúl.

6 The *grogue* distillery

Along the coast road on your return to Vila das Pombas, visit the archaic *trapiche* and taste some *grogue* at Senhor Ildo's distillery (*see p71*), entered through a battered old gate in the long white wall below the statue of St Anthony.
Follow the road back to Vila da Ribeira Grande.

The mountains running into the sea on the coast south of Ribeira Grande

The people and their language

Since the islands were uninhabited when they were discovered, the population grew from a handful of early European settlers and the many thousands of West Africans whom they captured as slaves to work the land; from the crews that manned the sailing ships on voyages of discovery, and the merchants, traders and adventurers who used and misused the islands down the centuries.

Among these were English, French, Spanish, Brazilians, Sephardic Jews, Lebanese, Moroccans, Dutch, Germans, Chinese and Americans, all of whom left their legacy. In today's diverse population are the descendants of slaves and slave traders, free men and refugees, exiles, dissidents and convicts.

Portuguese may be the official language of the country but Crioulo is the mother tongue. Containing a simplified grammar of 15th-century Portuguese, mainly that of the Algarve, mixed with words and phonetics from Fula, Mandingo and the myriad languages spoken by the communities of the West African mainland, Crioulo represents the very essence of Cape Verdean identity. It was created out of necessity. Thrown together in adversity, with their kaleidoscope of cultures and

The Cape Verdeans descend from many different peoples

Crioulo is spoken by everyone in Cape Verde

languages, the African slaves needed a viable method of communication. To add to their difficulties, their owners made every attempt to stop tribal languages being spoken. Punishments were harsh.

Out of the pidgin mix of Portuguese and Guinean used by slave owners to communicate with their labour force came a language that has grown and evolved differently from island to island, even between one part of an island and another.

Words and sayings often reflect the different nationalities that have influenced the islanders. The Crioulo spoken on São Vicente incorporates many English words; on Brava it is spattered with Americanisms. That spoken on the northern Barlavento group of islands differs quite markedly from the Sotavento Crioulo of the south. There is much rivalry, particularly between Santiago and São Vicente Crioulo speakers, and to settle on an accepted standard form would be impossible.

Crioulo is unlike any other Creole language spoken around the world and it is a spoken rather than a written language. Indeed, many Cape Verdeans cannot read or write it, and while it is the language of soulful poetry and *morna* songs, very few books have been published in Crioulo. Standardising the spelling has been one difficulty. The first attempt at an alphabet came in 1888, with a grammar based on Portuguese. Alupec (Unified Alphabet for Cape Verdean Writing) was devised in 1994.

In the mid-20th century, after 500 years under colonial rule when Cape Verde's inhabitants were classed as Portuguese/European, slave or *mestiço* (mixed race), a group of writers and intellectuals proposed the radical concept of Cape Verdean identity and nationhood, and fought for their beliefs. When independence came in 1975, the people of Cape Verde enthusiastically embraced their freedom to express pride in the culture, language and music so distinctly their own.

Santiago

While Santo Antão is the drama queen, Santiago displays its charms with a flowing grace. The largest and most populated of all the islands in the archipelago, and home to Praia, Cape Verde's capital and seat of government, Santiago is 55km (34 miles) long and 29km (18 miles) at its widest, with a surface area of 991sq km (383sq miles). It is one of the Sotavento (Leeward) group of islands and has a population of 280,000.

Two mountain ranges, with high craggy peaks and forests and terraced fields sweeping down their sides, rise up from the heart of the island. Wide valleys, farmed and gloriously green when the rains come, bisect them. In the southwest, nothing grows on the arid brown hills. The north has a good beach, while on the jagged eastern coast white-crested waves roll in to meet banana plantations.

Santiago is where the nation's history began. The Portuguese navigator Diogo Gomes and the Genoese António de Noli began settling the island in 1492. They brought slaves from the coast of West Africa to farm it, and started the lucrative businesses of resupplying ships and trading in slaves that would define Cape Verde for centuries. Not surprisingly, it is considered the most African of the islands.

Over half of the whole country's population lives on Santiago, and half of those live in Praia. The island has the best infrastructure on the archipelago, the country's only botanical gardens, the liveliest markets and the first European city in the tropics.

Scenic splendour

Scenically, Santiago seems to have it all: an array of volcanic mountains with cloud-raking peaks, tree-swathed red rock hills, wild plateaux and mosaics of tightly terraced fields cascading down steep hillsides. Along a serrated coastline, small bays are washed by white-crested waves. Villages snuggle into valleys and drape over hills. Banana fronds flap lazily in the breeze, coconut palms stand tall and mangoes and papayas ripen in the sunshine.

Everything about this island speaks of its history. It was the first to be settled, by a handful of Europeans and thousands of slaves, and their descendants haven't forgotten their ancestry. African traditions still hold strong and are especially evident in the vibrant music, colourful festivals and lively markets.

When pirates raided the coastal towns and caused chaos, some slaves, known as *badius*, seized the opportunity to run inland and hide in the mountains. Much later, freed slaves headed north in search of land they could farm and call their own, beginning their new lives around Assomada, 500m (1,640ft) up in the centre of the island. Now Santiago's second city, its thronged streets are distinctly African in character.

To see Santiago at its most beautiful, visit in the rainy season or just afterwards. September to December is generally the best time. Then the mountain slopes and wide valleys are a brilliant green and every turn in the road presents yet another stunning view.

Praia

The Plâto (Plateau), high above the port and bay, is where the city of Praia

Santiago *(see pp84–5 for orange route drive)*

Praia's lively market on Avenida 5 de Julho

began in the 18th century and is still its beating heart. A collection of districts and residential suburbs flows down its steep cliffs and across a level plain to the rocky coast and sandy bays below.

The imposing Parlamento (Parliament) building and the extravagant Chinese and Russian embassies vying for attention across the road are in Achada Santo António, along with some expensive housing and good restaurants. Just below it lies leafy Prainha, the upmarket district of hotels, embassies, ambassadorial residences and a popular local beach. The Chã d'Areia neighbourhood looks out across the harbour bay. To the southwest, smart new apartment blocks line the wider roads of Upper and Lower Palmarejo. Like many cities, the outskirts are poor. A jumble of shanty dwellings speaks of poverty and the migration from the countryside. Even for Cape Verde, which does not deal well with its garbage disposal problems, the fringes of the city are shockingly layered in litter.

On the Plâto, colonial Portuguese architecture lines busy streets and its main square is a quiet retreat fronting the old cathedral. Walk past the bank at the bottom of the square and around the Palácio da República to see a statue of explorer Diogo Gomes, one of the two men who discovered Santiago, and enjoy a grand view of the city and the sea.

On the traffic-jammed Avenida 5 de Julho you'll find the sights, sounds and smells of a typical African market. Clustered in a riot of colour against a cacophony of sound are mangoes and

TRIBUTE TO THE EMIGRANTS

'*Si ka badu, ka ta biradu*' – 'If you don't leave, you won't return'. The soothing words of Cape Verdean poet Eugénio Tavares are carved into the Monumento ao Emigrante, a tall sculpture on a roundabout outside Praia's international airport that reflects the history of Cape Verde and the debt the country owes to its diaspora. The abstract design of the monument, a white centrepiece on a stone background that signifies a ship, absorbs many symbols of departure and arrival. The base, a mosaic of blue and white, represents the waves of the sea that carried the early emigrants away, and the flowing white centre a waving handkerchief, reflecting the sadness of departure and the joy of arrival.

papayas, lemons and limes, yams and manioc. They pile up alongside fat tomatoes, juicy carrots, chubby sweet potatoes, firm cabbages, pungent spices and the herbs, dried leaves and strange roots used in the making of traditional remedies. Taking up a whole city centre block, this is also the place to buy lengths of brightly patterned material, jars of homemade sticky-sweet jams and, only if you have a very strong constitution, bottles of backyard-distilled *grogue*.

Museu Etnográfico de Praia (Museum of Ethnography)

In a beautifully restored colonial house, the Museum of Ethnography may be small but it has a fine collection of well-displayed artefacts. From examples of the finely woven *pano* cloth that harks back through the days of slavery through the clay pots, baskets and pestles and mortars used in the preparation of food, to the

Basketware on display in Praia's Museum of Ethnography

Fortaleza Real de São Filipe in Cidade Velha was built by the Portuguese in the 16th century

old musical instruments and wooden boats, the story of Cape Verdean life is told here.
Museum of Ethnography, Avenida 5 de Julho, Platô, Praia. Tel: 261 8421. Open: Mon–Fri 9.30am–noon & 2.30–5pm. Admission charge.

Núcleo Museológico (Underwater (Shipwreck) Museum)
Full of amazing finds from the days of sail, the Shipwreck Museum is tucked away at the back of an Armed Forces building. The treasures displayed here, dug from the depths of the ocean, include gold and silver coins, elephant tusks, ships' bells, astrolabes and a copper gimbals lamp. However, it is the personal items that are so touching: the brass luggage plate inscribed 'Miss Dixon', a passenger's gold-plated telescope complete with interchangeable lenses, fob watches, exquisite manicure sets and French cufflinks. There are also reminders of the cargos so many of these ships carried – bronze bracelet-like *manilas*, used as currency by European slave traders to purchase slaves in West Africa.
Núcleo Museologico da Praia, Cape Verde Telecom Street, Chã d'Areia, Praia. Tel: 261 8870. Open: Mon–Fri 9.30am–noon & 2.30–5pm. Admission charge.

Cidade Velha (Ribeira Grande)

Founded in 1462 as Ribeira Grande (Big Valley), and known for two centuries as Cidade Velha (Old City), in 2005 the city was officially renamed Cidade Ribeira Grande de Santiago. But nobody seems to have noticed. The first European city to be built in the tropics, it is a candidate for listing as a UNESCO World Heritage Site.

The arid southwest coast comes as a shock after seeing Santiago's lush green interior. The 10km (6-mile) drive from Praia is through a brown and bare landscape of high hills and distant mountains. Here the ground is too full of rocks and stones and the soil too poor to support agriculture, so the occasional flowering plant surprises with a sudden splash of colour.

You arrive first at the 16th-century **Fortaleza Real de São Filipe**. High on a hill above Cidade Velha, its silent cannons pointing seawards, there are grand views from the thick walls to the town spread out below and into the deep valley. Amazingly, given all the rock that surrounds it, the fort was constructed using stone and brick brought from Lisbon. Destroyed by pirate cannon fire, the cathedral that took 100 years to build stands in ruins on a plateau overlooking the sea.

The city was always subject to pirate attack, but it was two raids by Sir Francis Drake that caused the São Filipe fort to be built. Together with 1,000 men, Drake landed first in 1585 but, warned of his approach, the inhabitants fled to the mountains. He left after plundering the deserted city, and returned the following year when several ships were sunk during an intense naval battle. The interpretation centre at the restored fort, which has a café and small shop, tells its story (*open: daily 9am–5pm; free admission*).

Down in the little town it's hard to imagine how important, and how rich, it once was. From the 15th century onwards, Santiago proved a convenient staging post for the flourishing transatlantic slave trade. Captured Africans shipped to Cape Verde were sold to European slavers and dispatched to the Americas, north and south. Cidade Velha was at the heart of it all. Seventy years after it was first settled it was granted *cidade* (city) status, and by 1572 had a population of over 1,500, the majority of them slaves working in the valley plantations.

Today the main square, lined with old houses and affording sea views at its far end, is a busy atmospheric little place. Yet it was here that thousands of African slaves were bought and sold. At its centre, a carved marble pillar looks innocent enough until you get closer and see the iron rings. Erected in 1512, this was the *pelourinho* where slaves were publicly flogged.

Two rows of whitewashed stone houses with thatched roofs sit among palm trees at the mouth of the valley where long ago a stream delivered the water that replenished thousands of visiting ships. A report from 1545 detailed 'more than 500 houses made of stone where uncountable numbers of Spanish and Portuguese Knights live'. Walk among them and into Rua de Banana to reach the church of **Nossa Senhora do Rosário**. Dating from 1495, it's the oldest church in Cape Verde. Outside there's the tombstone of Nicolau Gomes Ferreira, one of Cidade Velha's most popular priests. He is rumoured to have fathered 40 children. The dates of his birth and death are obscured, but those of his brother, buried alongside him, are 1850–1933.

There's a pleasant walk up into the *ribeira* (valley) among the trees and banana plantations. Although it looks lush and green after rain, it must have been much more fertile back in the early days. An account written in the 16th century described the upper valley as having vast groves of oranges, lemons, pomegranates, figs and coconut palms.

In 1712, the notorious French pirate Jacques Cassart robbed Cidade Velha of all its riches, causing such devastation that the city had to be abandoned. By 1724, a more easily defendable city had arisen further east along the coast. Praia became the capital of Santiago and Cidade Velha was left to decay.

Recognition of Cidade Velha's historical importance, and its tourism potential, is bringing the crumbling little town to life again. Old colonial houses have been spruced up and given preservation orders, new restaurants are opening, and hotels and a resort development are under construction along the coast.

Tarrafal

The centre of Tarrafal is laid out around a big square, overseen by the imposing blue-and-white façade of the church, but the main attraction here is the wide sandy beach. It curves into a bay with hills and a rocky headland providing a sheltering arm.

At weekends the beach is packed with families and groups of friends, their associated picnics, barbecues and football games played out to a reggae beat. Go in the morning when the fishermen pull up with their catch and a drama unfolds as a scramble of women clusters around the boats, arguing noisily over the price. Deals done, they set off across the sand with a big bowl of still writhing fish balanced on their heads.

Tarrafal is pretty sleepy and there's a limited choice of places to stay, but it's good for a night or two relaxing by the sea. Moreover, the two- to three-hour drive there, along snaking roads through the centre of the island, is spectacular (*see pp84–7*).

Museu de Resistência (Resistance Museum)

Surrounded by four guard towers and dotted with sentry boxes, the long low buildings have the look of an old army camp. Yet the former prison between the village of Chão Bom (Good Land) and the outskirts of Tarrafal was once known as the 'slow death camp'.

The Tarrafal concentration camp was set up under the orders of the Portuguese dictator António de Oliveira Salazar in 1936 to house opponents of his fascist regime. Under the control of the notorious Secret Police, hundreds of people were held there and severely tortured. Yellow fever, and the malaria-carrying mosquitoes from the nearby swamp, finished off many of the badly weakened prisoners.

International pressure led to the camp being closed in 1956, but it opened again in 1961 to incarcerate African resistance fighters from the Portuguese colonial wars. It finally closed in 1974 after the fall of the Lisbon regime. The old buildings have been restored and a museum created to tell its gruesome history and remember the people who suffered and died there. *Museu de Resistência, Chão Bom, Tarrafal. Tel: 266 6826. Open: most days, but phone to check times. Admission charge.*

A reminder of its slave-trading history, a carved marble pillar, the *pelhourinho*, stands in Cidade Velha's main square

Drive: Santiago's scenic highlights

Explore high mountains, green valleys and a jagged coastline on this route around the island.

See page 77 for map.

The drive is 150km (93 miles) and it can be done in a day from Praia, but an overnight stay along the route would be ideal.

Leave Praia on the good asphalt road north that sweeps through low hills and acacia plantations. Heading for São Domingos, it swings through tree-sloped mountains, past fields of manioc, cabbages, mango and papaya trees and small settlements on the hillsides.

A potter at work in São Domingos

1 São Domingos

A small but busy little town where traditional crafts are being revived in a community project. The Centro Artesanatos ceramics workshop is on the main road in the centre of São Domingos. Here you can watch potters at work at their wheels and skilled weavers at narrow wooden looms working on the intricate patterns of *pano*. This fine cloth, woven by African slaves, was so highly prized that it was used as currency by the traders at the coast. A slave was worth 60 *pano* cloths, each 2m by 18cm (3ft by 7in). You can see a collection of the colourful wares in the studio shop.

Turn left at the sign 'Quinta da Montanha', taking the cobbled road that winds up to Rui Vaz.

2 Quinta da Montanha

This is a scenic drive into the mountains, their sides steeply terraced, where every inch of the red-brown earth seems to be cultivated. Ahead lies Pico d'Antónia, at 1,394m (4,573ft) the highest peak on the island. Watch out for the elusive Bourne's Heron, found only on Cape Verde, which makes its home in this area. A lane lined with blowsy red hibiscus bushes leads to the Quinta da Montanha rural retreat (*see p156*), the ideal place for a coffee or lunch on the terrace, with panoramic views over the valley.

Return to the main road, turn left and drive to João Teves village. There take the left turn marked 'São Jorge dos Orgãos' which leads up to the Botanical Gardens.

3 Jardim Botânico Nacional (National Botanical Gardens)

In a verdant valley under towering mountains, the INIDA agricultural research centre has a botanical garden where endemic and introduced species are studied and work is being done on conserving species threatened with extinction. The Cape Verde Warbler can be spotted here. Continue upwards on a rough track to the *miradores* (high viewpoint) from where the entire valley spreads out before you. *Grogue* is distilled in the villages dotting the valley sides.

Head back to the main road and turn left towards Assomada, passing Picos, a small town sitting on a ridge jutting out between the surrounding deep valleys. The Salvador do Mundo (Saviour of the World) music festival held there at the end of April attracts visitors from all over Santiago and beyond.

4 Assomada

Santiago's bustling second city is home to around 55,000 people. A market is

The Botanical Gardens are a centre for the preservation of endangered species

held here daily but the big days are Wednesdays and Saturdays, a tradition that dates back to the 19th century. Then it seems that half the island is in Assomada to buy and sell. When slavery officially ended in 1876, freed slaves moved into the mountains, building stone walls around their houses for fear of being taken back into slavery. Many of the women you see here wear twisted *pano* cloth strung around their waists and resting on their hips, a tradition dating back to the days of slavery. After Praia, it's the most African of all Cape Verde's towns and cities.

Outside Assomada the road becomes cobbled (watch out for the speed bumps!). Drive through Achada Falcão, a fast-developing town with a new high school and regional hospital, and on into the high mountains.

Neatly terraced fields climb Santiago's steep hill and mountain slopes

5 Serra Malagueta

In this national park of high peaks, the air is cool and the views are spectacular. Troops of wild green monkeys hide in crevices and cause havoc to the crops grown by the subsistence farmers in the area. Women balancing huge bundles of firewood on their heads climb the steep slopes to their homes.

On the other side of the mountains, the valley on the right is Ribeira Principal, its sides neatly terraced, its base planted with sugar cane and mango trees. There's a top-of-the-world feeling as you drive along ridges with steep drops. Red-roofed houses in traditional Portuguese style dot the slopes around Achada Lengueira, where the vertical terraces are amazing.

Turn left and drive through the fast-expanding little town of Chão Bom, stopping to visit the Resistance Museum in the former prison (see pp82–3) before heading for the beach at Tarrafal.

6 Tarrafal

Fishing boats line up at one end of the sandy beach, palm trees and little bungalows at the other. Curving into a sheltered bay with a rocky headland and backed by mountains, this is a very popular spot at weekends. For a refreshing drink, buy a coconut from the fruit sellers in the car park off the main square. Nearby, the Baía Verde restaurant overlooking the beach is a good place for lunch (*see p156*).

Drive back towards Praia along the coast road.

The popular beach at Tarrafal

7 Espinho Branco

The cobbled coast road climbs and falls above a cobalt sea foaming against black volcanic rocks. It dips inland, where plants struggle in the red earth and acacia trees are bowed by Saharan winds. At Porto Formoso, coconut palms edge a stony beach in a cove backed by banana fronds and sugar cane. In the nearby village, pigs snuffle among stones, and goats and chickens have little road sense.

About 3km (1¾ miles) after Mangue de Sete Ribeiras bay, where fingers of rock reach into the sea, look out for the hilltop Rabelados settlement (*see pp88–9*) in Espinho Branco. A rough track on the right leads up to the small studio shop that displays and sells their intriguing naïve paintings.

Continue along the coast road towards Praia.

8 Pedra Badejo

After a series of small towns where all life is lived on the streets, banana plantations cover the wide flat finish to a *ribeira* (valley) as it opens out to the sea. A dense reforestation project of acacia trees lines and shades the road as it heads up and down hills, through small settlements and past houses with dark interiors. At Pedra Badejo take the left turn into the town, where the fishing harbour is busy and children delight in jumping off the rocks into the sea. There's a boat-shaped café at the water's edge.

Return to the main road. The route now is entirely inland, passing banana plantations, tall palm trees and small towns set against a backdrop of mountain layers and hills outlined by trees. When the cobbled road meets asphalt turn left, then it's 10km (6 miles) to Praia.

The Rabelados

Buffeted by Harmattan winds blowing straight from the Sahara, a cluster of woven palm houses look out over the Atlantic from a rocky outcrop at Espinho Branco, on Santiago's east coast. Women till the stony earth, chickens scratch at the dusty ground, goats forage for anything they can find. There's a handwritten sign now, directing visitors up a track to the hilltop 'studio' displaying colourful, highly distinctive, naïve paintings. It wasn't always so. Until recently this little community, part of a group known as Rabelados, shunned all contact with the outside world.

Rabelados artworks on display

The Rabelados ('Rebels' in Crioulo) are a religious people. Descendents of runaway African slaves who hid in the mountains, surviving against the odds in inhospitable terrain and clinging to the traditions of their homelands, they hold God and their Christian religion at the centre of their lives. They live simply, farming their land communally, sharing each other's burdens.

The rebellion that gave them their name came in 1941, with the arrival in Cape Verde of Portuguese 'white cassock' priests from the Congregation of the Holy Spirit. Appalled by the secular lifestyle of the local Catholic priests, whose congregations expected them to father children, and traditional rituals and practices they considered pagan, they set about bringing 'true' Roman Catholicism to the islands, persecuting all who deviated from their teachings.

Already shunned by a society that didn't understand their isolated way of life, when the Rabelados formed

Cape Verdean artist Misa encourages young Rabelados in their art and promotes their work abroad

tight groups to practise the old religion in secret they were rooted out, their leaders jailed and individual members of the movement banished to different points around the islands. During the liberation wars that raged in Portugal's African colonies, they were denounced as political activists, and suffered incarceration in the notorious Tarrafal prison (*see p82*).

Independence from Portugal brought the Rabelados what they wanted – recognition of their identity as a group and the freedom to practise their religion. They still venerate the old PAIGC flag, a symbol of the party that delivered the independence and formed the first Cape Verdean government.

Having spurned the march of progress for so long, the Rabelados are adapting to the modern world. Their children now attend local schools and some families are building new houses from breezeblocks, in line with the rest of Cape Verde. Older members of the community, however, still favour *funko*, the airy two-roomed, straw-roofed homes crafted from woven coconut palm leaves on a frame of thin logs. 'God should be able to move freely', they say.

The Espinho Branco community has a young man at its head. Tchetcho was 24 when his father died in 2006 and he succeeded to the leadership. The following year he travelled to Spain to promote the art that is giving the Rabelados an international presence and to receive help to support the village. The art project is run by Maria Isabel Alves, known to all as Misa, a Cape Verdean artist with an international reputation who has lived most of her life in Switzerland. Having discovered artistic talent among young Rabelados, she provides paper, paints and a great deal of encouragement and support, as well as promoting their work abroad.

Fogo

Fogo means 'Fire' in Crioulo, an apt name for the island that's actually an awesome, and still active, volcano. At 2,829m (9,280ft), Pico de Fogo is the highest point in Cape Verde. Originally called São Filipe in honour of the saint on whose day the island was discovered in 1460, and still the name of its main town, it was renamed Fogo in 1680 after a devastating eruption that lit the skies for years. Fogo lies 50km (31 miles) west of Santiago and was the second island to be settled.

Rising from the sea with dark slopes tapering to a crowning cone, Fogo looks like the archetypal image of a volcano. Round in shape with a surface area of 476sq km (184sq miles), the island has dry and arid zones in the south, while the humid north is green and fertile. One of the Sotavento (Leeward) group, it is the hottest and most humid island in the archipelago and is home to around 40,000 people.

Fogo was settled soon after Santiago. By 1582, 100 Europeans controlled a workforce of 13,700 slaves who toiled in the fields and cotton plantations of the two islands. Many were skilled weavers, and the cloth they produced was highly prized in Africa and Brazil. After an attack by Dutch pirates in 1655, Lisbon's only response to a call for more European settlers was to ship in some convicts.

Built on a cliff above black sand beaches and pounding surf, the main town of São Filipe has a faded grandeur. Its squares and wide avenues are lined with colonial mansions known as *sobrados*. But it is the fascination of the inhabited volcano that draws visitors to Fogo.

The awesome volcano

All the Cape Verde islands are volcanic, but Fogo, being the baby at a mere 100,000 years or so old, is the only one that leaves you in no doubt about its origins. Its volcano towers dark and forbidding above the towns and villages on its slopes. Inside its vast crater, which is about 10km (6 miles) long and 7km (4 miles) wide, the giant caldera floor is littered with the eruptions of past centuries. Thus, the crater bears the title Chã das Caldeiras (Plain of Craters).

Volcanologists believe it was originally 3,500m (11,500ft) high, and that some time in the last 10,000 years part of its steep eastern walls collapsed, reducing its height considerably.
A massive eruption in 1680 smothered fields, sending those inhabitants who

could flee to neighbouring Brava. The fires that gave the island its new name could be seen for miles. Indeed, ships used the island as a navigational aid until well into the 1700s.

In 1785, Pico de Fogo erupted and flowing lava formed the bulge in the coastline on which the town of Mosteiros now sits. Since then, all of the eruptions have been within the ancient crater. The most recent was in April 1995. Preceded by a series of warning earthquakes, a line of fissures split the Pico. Curtains of fire ripped across the crater and clouds of dark ash rising 5km (3 miles) into the sky engulfed the whole island. Lava continued flowing for two months.

New houses were built on the southern slopes for the people who had been living in the crater at the time, but they didn't stay. Today, the crater villages of Portela and Bangaeira are home to about 1,500 people. There's a small hotel, bar and restaurant in Portela, alongside a wine-producing cooperative and a pizzeria with Internet access.

Fogo

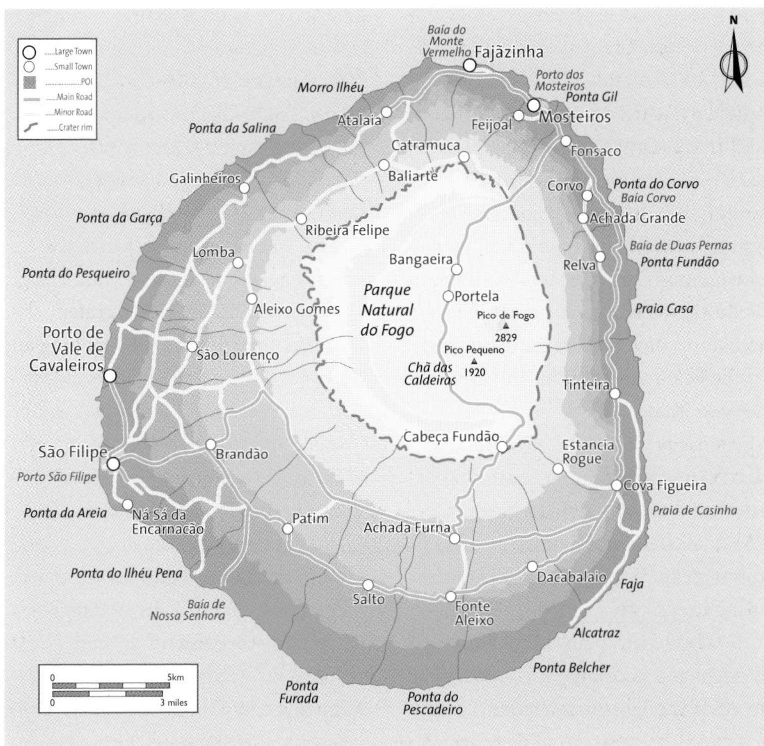

Pico de Fogo, the highest point on Cape Verde

Road to the top

A bumpy cobbled road leaves São Filipe through stands of acacia trees, planted to help control erosion. Maize, beans, manioc, potatoes and peanuts grow in irrigated fields flanked by bananas and mango trees. The heat and humidity of the town are left behind as the road climbs steadily upwards through deeply furrowed terrain, and the air feels fresher and cooler.

The route circles the volcano's southern slopes, passing isolated villages where goat's cheese is produced and there are smallholdings of cows and pigs. Terraces of stony fields sit against a backdrop of sweeping red-brown hills. After rain, a fine grass springs up and colours the red earth a shade of pale green and breathes new life into the landscape. Wide rivers of lava, formed by the eruptions of earlier centuries, add ever more texture to the scene.

Concreted slopes, like sturdy white handkerchiefs propped up against the hillside, catch rainwater and guide it into channels that feed into storage tanks. The water collected is used to irrigate fields and grow a surprising variety of crops. This is based on the Portuguese *levada* system, for which the island of Madeira is so famous.

Then you are on a dizzying upward climb of hairpin bends and fantastic views from the road, all the way down to the coast. At Cabeça Fundão, the last settlement before the caldera, a huddle of flat-roofed lava-brick houses is built into the mountainside, their pride and joy a concrete sports field. Here, getting the ball back is not an option. Sisal plants edge the road as yet another bend above a deep crevasse reveals the magnificent peak and a sign welcomes you to the Parque Natural do Fogo.

Chã das Caldeiras

Entering the vast crater is an other-worldly experience. A well-worn track crosses its silent, gritty black heart and high jagged walls rise up in an amphitheatre of craggy mountains. A series of strangely shaped cones, some of them nearing 2,000m (6,560ft) high, tell of a turbulent and fiery history. The yellow-streaked and charred-looking one on the right is the newest addition to the Chã das Caldeiras collection. Called Pico Pequeno (Little

VINES OF THE CHÃ

Each vine is planted in a shallow dip dug into ground consisting of small, solidified fragments of lava known as *lapilli*. Moisture, which gathers on the rock at night and condenses, dribbles into the holes to provide the water the vines need for growth.
Red, white and rosé wines are made at the Cooperativo in Portela, a village inside the crater. They carry the 'Chã' label and have an alcohol content of 14 per cent. Spirits ('Espiritos da Caldeira', 45 per cent alcohol) are also distilled there using island-grown fruits, including grape (*grappa*), quince, apple and peach, and a herbal *digestif*.

Peak), it was formed during the 1995 eruption and is 1,920m (6,300ft) high. The great Pico de Fogo towers above them all, dominating all it surveys.

A walk around Portela village reveals a school and a sports field, grey lava-brick houses, a tiny general store and a health centre, plus the all-important cooperative that produces wine from the vines grown on the crater rim. There's also a bar, an Italian restaurant, and a shop selling Chã wines, fruit preserves and souvenirs crafted from lava stone. Stubby vegetation clings to life on cinder slopes, and there are even a few trees. Loudspeakers strung along the street are a reminder that the peaceful existence here could one day be shattered. If the volcano shows signs of activity, Portela's residents will get the message loud and clear.

You can see Bangaeira, the second crater village, in the distance below.

The wine cooperative in Chã das Caldeiras

This is the starting point for a 10km (6-mile) hike that passes grape vines and a small forest, then goes over the crater rim into a steep descent all the way to the coast at Mosteiros. This scenic route encompasses lush vegetation, deep ravines, tiny villages, orange groves, coffee plantations and some mesmerising views.

São Filipe

The centre of São Filipe may feel quite small, but it is the fifth largest town in Cape Verde and has the designation of *cidade* (city). It is the country's second oldest settlement after Cidade Velha in Santiago. The inhabitants of Fogo are the descendants of families from the Algarve and Alentejo in Portugal, and their slaves.

Built on a hill, the steep tree-lined streets and flowery squares end at a cliff above long, black-sanded beaches pounded by a powerful blue sea.

São Filipe is an attractive and colourful town that wears its colonial history on its sleeve. Its historic centre has some beautiful *sobrados* (literally, 'wooden floors'), houses that were the homes of rich, slave-owning Portuguese landowners. Many of them have been lovingly restored (*see p97*).

Painted in soft pastel shades or warm ochre, with their wood-shuttered windows and balconies, they look elegantly out onto cobbled avenues and spacious squares. Decorated with the finest woods from Africa and tiles brought from Portugal, these gracious two-storey homes have interior courtyards planted with trees and bright flowers. Originally the ground floor was used for business. The family lived on the balconied first floor, in rooms overlooking the courtyard on three sides. Some houses had two courtyards. These were used for storing seed and produce, rainwater in cisterns and for stabling thoroughbred horses that the owner rode in festivals. Slaves were allowed upstairs just once a year, on 3 May, the festival of Santa Cruz.

THE FECUND DUKE

In the caldera, you'll meet children with blue eyes, ginger-blonde hair and complexions the shade of milky coffee. The pale-skinned people of the volcano can trace their ancestry back to an eccentric French duke, François Louis Armand Montrond.

When he landed in Cape Verde en route for Brazil in 1872, the Duke of Montrond was so taken with the islands that he stayed, settling in Fogo's crater. Exactly how many children he fathered is uncertain, but his descendants are countless. Putting his engineering experience to good use, he had Fogo's first road built and sank wells. He is also credited with importing the vines that started Fogo's wine production.

Casa da Memória

The furnished rooms of one of São Filipe's beautifully renovated *sobrados* display household items, ceramics and kitchenware in everyday use during the 19th century when the house was built, as well as old photographs and personal memorabilia. The house is both a

privately run museum and cultural centre. In the 1960s, its courtyard was used as the town's cinema.
Casa da Memória, Praça Câmara Municipal (Town Hall Square), São Filipe. Tel: 281 2765. Open: Wed, Thur & Fri 10am–noon, or by appointment. Admission charge.

The fertile north

To see just how fertile volcanic soil can be, you need to go north to Mosteiros. The road there from São Filipe goes along the east coast, and is particularly scenic from **Cova Figueira**, a small town of colourful, neatly kept houses with terraced fields tumbling steeply down to the sea.

From there, the road zigzags along at the feet of mountains, with the coastline always in view. Sisal sprouts from sheer rock faces, mango trees fruit among lava and long valleys are planted with maize. Cows and goats find pasture in dips and gullies. The great lava stream at **Tinteira** looks menacing.

There are great crevices gouged through the mountainside where men hoe land of ankle-breaking difficulty. A little white chapel sits completely alone overlooking the sea, isolated at the end of a lava field. At wild and bleak **Relva**, houses perch way up high and pigs live in circular rock-piled sties.

Between mountain and sea, smouldering in the humidity, **Mosteiros** lies under forbidding rock among palm trees. New houses are painted in cheerful colours, a welcome contrast to Fogo's traditional dark lava-block homes. There was an airport here once, the outline of its runway still visible from the road winding up into the mountains. Steep hills are intensely cultivated, right into ravines slipping headlong towards the sea.

Fogo's fertile north is magnificent. Cloud drifts through velvet green mountain folds above banana and coffee plantations, peach, mango, apple and quince trees, citrus groves and fields of vegetables. All are revealed from a roller-coaster road crossing the top of the island in the shadow of the volcano.

Bananas are among many crops grown in the fertile north of Fogo island

Walk: Historic São Filipe

With its cobbled streets lined with trees and splendid squares filled with hibiscus and oleander shrubs, São Filipe is a pleasing town full of life and history. This downhill walk takes in the highlight of sobrados, *grand homes built by rich Portuguese families during the 19th century.*

Allow two hours as the walk covers about 3km (1¾ miles).

Begin at the Aquadinha, the water distribution centre.

1 Aquadinha

The Aquadinha is a rather grand orange-painted building with a stone carved bust of João de Figueiredo, a former Governor of Cape Verde, in its gardens. Past the Shell petrol station, the post office is on your left and on your right is a clothes market.

Following the right side of traffic-busy Cruz de Paz, when you see the papelaria *(stationer's shop) on a corner, turn right.*

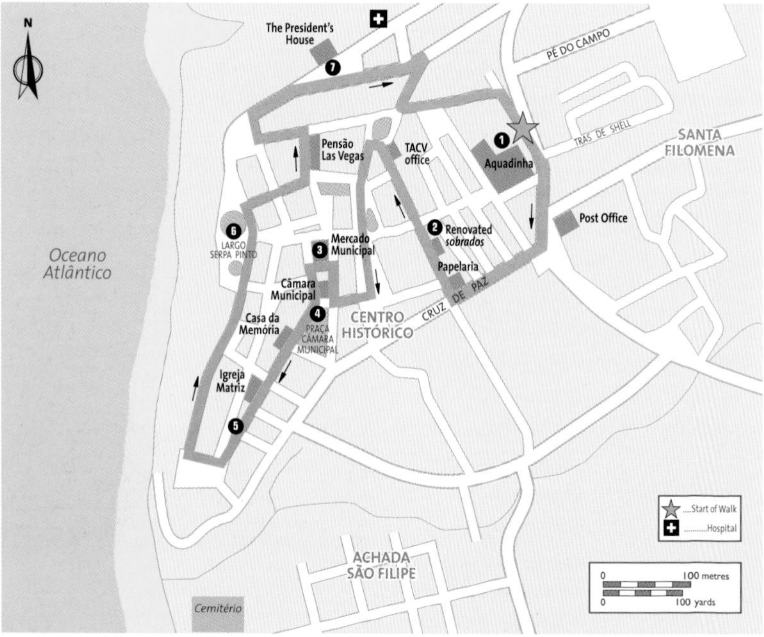

A renovated *sobrado* in São Filipe

2 Renovated *sobrados*

Two formerly rundown *sobrados* have been restored to their former glory on this street of restaurants and bars. The Tropical Club and Cyber Café boasts a courtyard shaded by a giant tree. At the end of the street, turn left at the TACV office. (Looking right, up the hill, you'll see the Pousada Belavista, a good place to stay in town, *see p157.*) Two large *sobrados* face each other on the corner approaching a square, one with a traditional roof-tiled veranda upstairs. Keeping left, the blue wall of Le Bistrot (*see p157*) is topped by a terrace, ideal for a short rest and refreshment.

Cross the square by the bright orange Loja Chinês Boutique and turn right, passing alongside the peeling blue Câmara Municipal (Town Hall), to the Mercado Municipal (Town Market).

3 The market

Here the fresh fruits and vegetables of the island are arrayed on stalls inside the busy covered market hall. Outside, the market traders spill out onto the cobbled street, where a sign on the wall of the Maria Amélia Pensão Bar Restaurante pronounces 'The best food in town' and the *pensão* offers a hairdressing and manicure salon.

Walk through the market and turn left into the Praça Câmara Municipal (Town Hall Square).

4 Praça Câmara Municipal (Town Hall Square)

This splendid square is lined with restored *sobrados* in many shades, from palest pastel to earthy ochre, all with tiny balconies under their shuttered windows. At the bottom of the square

The beach and colonial cemetery at São Filipe

on the right, the Casa da Memória is an old colonial family home that is now a small museum of Fogo memorabilia (*see pp94–5*). The size and spaciousness of a *sobrado* was an indication of the wealth and importance of its owner, who would also have had a similar house in the country, surrounded by trees and large gardens, where the family spent the hot summers overseeing their farms.

Continue down into the next square where you'll find the Igreja Matriz, the Mother Church.

5 Sea views

The impressive twin-towered church, renovated in 2007, is painted in turquoise blue and iced with white, and dominates the square, which is again lined with *sobrados*. One of them, the stylishly renovated Casa Renate, has apartments for holiday rental. The houses on this square were the first to be built in São Filipe and date from the mid-18th century.

Ahead is the clifftop promenade, literally the end of the road, where the Restaurante Seafood Bar has grand ocean views but not much seafood on the menu (*see p157*). The island of Brava sits on the horizon.

To your left, a road leads down to the long, black sand beach, buffeted by Atlantic rollers, that stretches far along the coast in both directions. Atop its cliffs, the old prison has a fine view of the sea and it looks straight across at the cemetery on the clifftop opposite, which must have been thought provoking for its inmates. The cemetery, now closed, is a remnant from colonial days when it was preserved purely for the island's Portuguese residents.

Walk up the narrow lane at the far side of the promenade, passing alongside a bakery where bread and pastries are baked in a traditional beehive-shaped oven. Go right, through a passage between two houses, and continue to a large square, Largo Serpa Pinto.

6 Largo Serpa Pinto

This big colonial-style square on two levels is the scene of a major two-day festival, Bandeira (Flag) de São Filipe, held every year on 30 April and 1 May. The event is packed with symbolism, processions, much feasting, singing, drumming and dancing. Associated sporting activities include football matches, horse racing and sailing contests.

Turn right at the top of the square, then turn left and walk past a couple of nightclubs and bars and a row of low, Portuguese-style homes. Turning left opposite the Pensão Las Vegas will lead you into São Filipe's wide main street.

7 The President's House

Lined with impressive houses along the hill down towards the sea – the green one next to the church is owned by the President of Cape Verde, Pedro Pires – this wide street houses the courthouse, banks, a hospital and the primary school.

Climb up to the top of the street, turn right, then right again, and make your way back to the Aquadinha.

São Filipe's church has been lovingly renovated

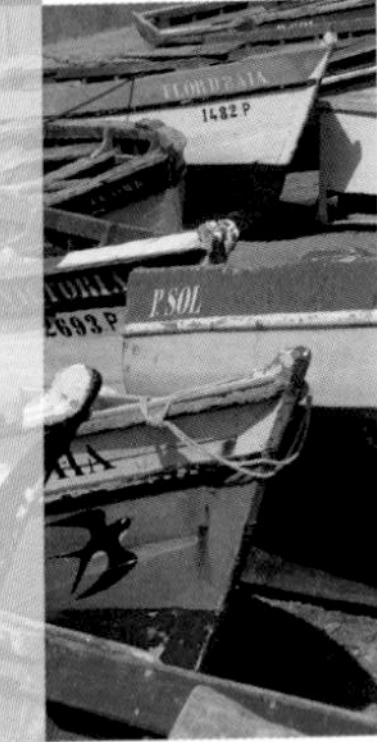

São Nicolau

Famed for its writers and thinkers, São Nicolau was Cape Verde's seat of learning. A strangely shaped island, one of the Barlavento (Windward) group, it stretches for 50km (31 miles) east to west and is 25km (15½ miles) at its widest. Most of the landscape is arid and dry, but at the heart of São Nicolau lie spectacular green mountains that are perfect for hiking. This is one of the most impressive islands in the archipelago, yet it's hardly been touched by tourism.

Viewed from the air and the sea, São Nicolau looks barren and inhospitable. However, it hides a secret, for inside those tough-looking mountains and volcanic peaks lies a heart of green. Even Vila de Ribeira Brava, the pretty little main town, sits tucked up at the base of a deep, steep-sided valley.

Two mountain ranges meet at Monte Gordo, the highest peak at 1,312m

São Nicolau (*see pp106–7 for orange route drive*)

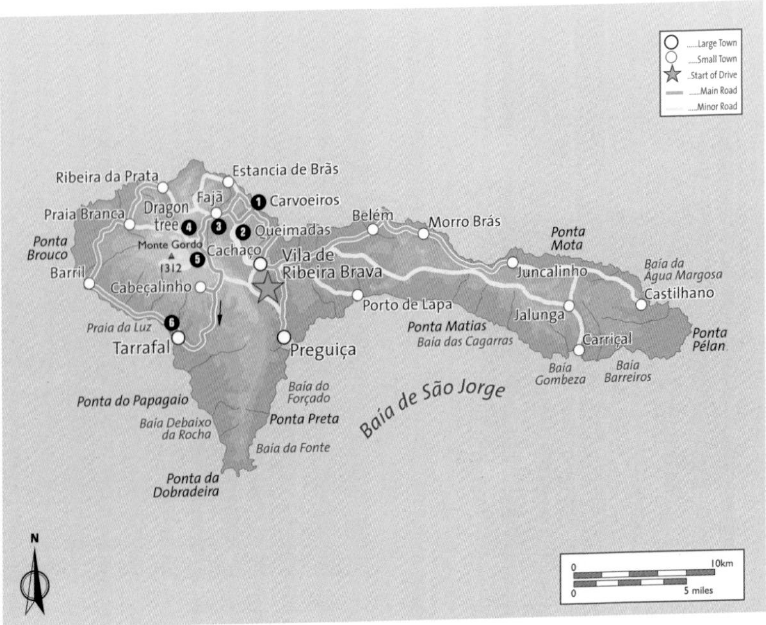

Large Town
Small Town
Start of Drive
Main Road
Minor Road

Ribeira da Prata
Estancia de Brãs
Fajã
1 Carvoeiros
Praia Branca
Dragon tree 4
3
2 Queimadas
Belém
Morro Brás
Ponta Brouco
Monte Gordo 1312
5
Cachaço
Vila de Ribeira Brava
Ponta Mota
Barril
Cabeçalinho
Juncalinho
Baía da Água Margosa
Castilhano
Porto de Lapa
Praia da Luz
6
Tarrafal
Preguiça
Ponta Matias
Baía das Cagarras
Jalunga
Carriçal
Ponta Pélan
Baía Gombeza
Baía Barreiros
Baía de São Jorge
Baía do Forçado
Ponta do Papagaio
Baía Debaixo da Rocha
Ponta Preta
Baía da Fonte
Ponta da Dobradeira
N
0 10km
0 5 miles

(4,305ft). This has been designated a protected natural park and is considered one of the most pristine areas in Cape Verde. Small villages hug hillsides where the inhabitants farm sugar cane and brew *grogue*. Bananas, guavas, passion fruit and papayas thrive in the hot and humid Fajã Valley. Down at the bare and brutal coast, where giant tuna fish are landed daily, the dark volcanic sands of Tarrafal are said to have healing properties and to bring relief to arthritis sufferers.

São Nicolau is home to the endangered Dragon tree (*Dracaena draco*) that lives at high altitudes, grows up to 10m (33ft) tall and is reputed to be able to live for 1,000 years. Known locally as *dragoeiro*, it looks prehistoric. While it used to be found on several Cape Verde islands, São Nicolau seems to be the only one where it still grows naturally.

A slow start

The first people to inhabit the island after it was discovered on St Nicholas' Day, 6 December 1461, arrived from Madeira in 1510. They set up home in Porto de Lapa on the coast, where the long, pointing finger of barren mountains forms the archipelago's widest bay, the Baía de São Jorge. There they farmed, growing maize, beans and cotton, and raised pigs, goats and cows, selling the produce, meat and hides to the sailing ships that called in to Cape Verde for supplies.

Although only a small community, the bay and its safe anchorage proved

Small farms such as these at Queimadas dot the green valleys of the interior

Ribeira Brava sits at the foot of the mountains

attractive to marauding pirates, and by the mid-17th century Porto de Lapa had been abandoned in favour of the safer interior of the island at Ribeira Brava. Pirates continued to raid until a fort was built at Preguiça in 1818 to defend the bay.

It took a long time to attract settlers to São Nicolau. A report despatched in 1683 noted the vineyards, an abundance of trees and a great number of goats and donkeys, but only 100 families. By 1731, Ribeira Brava was home to just 260 people. The population grew after the defensive fort promised more security.

Today around 20,000 people live on the island, relying on agriculture and fishing for a living. Ribeira Brava is the administrative centre, but fast-growing Tarrafal on the coast is the biggest town on São Nicolau.

Vila de Ribeira Brava

Linked by steep cobbled streets, Ribeira Brava's houses stack up on the rocky sides of the valley. They look down over the pleasing little town of prettily painted buildings with white shutters and red-tiled roofs, flower-filled gardens and two spacious squares.

The main square is watched over by an imposing church, a memorial to local philanthropist Dr Julio José Dias, and the town's library, which is housed in an old colonial home.

With its fine altar, painted ceiling and stained-glass windows, the **Igreja Matriz de Nossa Senhora do Rosário** is the most impressive church in Cape Verde. Dating from the early 18th century, it was rebuilt as a cathedral in the 1890s. São Nicolau was the seat of the bishopric from 1866 until 1940, when it moved to São Vicente.

A narrow street of lovely colonial houses painted in shades of ochre, turquoise and cream leads into the second square where the elegant Câmara Municipal (Town Hall) is distinctly colonial Portuguese in style. Facing it, the modern post office is fronted by flower-filled gardens with benches placed under shady trees. The statue in the gardens is of Baltasar Lopes da Silva, one of Cape Verde's most revered poets who died in 1989.

Behind the Câmara Muncipal (Town Hall) are more gardens, filled with shady trees and bright flowers. Across the dry riverbed and up a steep hill to the left, the old seminary from which so much learning emerged has been attractively renovated but is closed.

The town centre's two main streets, just wide enough for a constant stream of minibus *alugueres* to drive through, lead down from the church. They do have names (Rua Capitão João de Deus Lopes da Silva and Rua Dr Baltazar Lopes da Silva) but are simply known as 'Right Street' and 'Left Street' – a definition that changes depending on which direction you are facing at the time. There's a market on the main square and small shops that sell a surprising variety of goods from their dark interiors.

If you've come from windy, litter-strewn Sal or big city Praia, the first thing you'll probably notice about Ribeira Brava, and again while travelling around the island, is how clean and tidy it is.

In the week leading up to the start of Lent (February or March, depending on the date of Easter), quiet little Ribeira Brava takes on a whole new character. Carnival is a huge celebration, second only to Mindelo in its lavishness and fun, and the partying goes on non-stop for four days.

Seat of learning

That São Nicolau became the centre of higher education in the 19th and early 20th centuries was thanks to Cape Verde's first medical doctor, Dr Julio José Dias. The son of a wealthy landowner, he studied at the Sorbonne in Paris and gained some fame in

A memorial to philanthropist Dr Julio José Dias in front of the library in Ribeira Brava

Europe before returning to work on his native island. In 1866, he offered his mansion in Ribeira Brava to a group of Portuguese priests looking to found a seminary on Cape Verde. It was to be the first high school in Portuguese Africa and in all West Africa.

For the first time, bright Cape Verdean and African children had the opportunity to study at the same level as their counterparts in Portugal, a classical education that prepared them for careers in the Church and the Portuguese civil service. Serving as priests, teachers and administrators, they were highly influential in Portugal's colonies and spawned another generation of thinkers and activists, some of whom would be instrumental in changing the face of the African continent. National hero Amílcar Cabral, who was the son of a seminary-educated teacher, led the liberation struggle in Guinea-Bissau (*see pp16–17*).

However, when Church and State were separated in 1911 during

'SODADE'

'Sodade', the song that propelled Cesária Évora to international fame and has become a trademark of the islands, was written by Armando Zeferino Soares, who lived in the isolated village of Praia Branca among the mountains of northwest São Nicolau. The Crioulo word *sodade* means 'nostalgia' or 'yearning', and Soares wrote his haunting song in the sad poetic *morna* tradition on the day he bid farewell to some São Nicolau friends leaving in search of work on São Tomé and Principe in the 1950s. Musical farewells were common then, and reflected the sadness at leaving when there seemed little likelihood of return. Soares died in 2007 at the age of 87.

Locals fetching water in the island's interior

One of the ancient Dragon trees

Portugal's period as a parliamentary republic, the knock-on effect was to part the São Nicolau seminary from its high school, which moved to Mindelo on São Vicente. The seminary closed in 1917, reopened for a few years in the 1920s, and finally closed in 1931.

The poet and writer Baltasar Lopes da Silva, born in 1907, is probably São Nicolau's most famous son. He was one of the founders of the literary movement that published *Claridade,* which promoted Cape Verdean identity and culture, a revolutionary prospect in the 1930s. His novel *Chiquinho,* published in 1947, was the first to explore the reality of life on the islands, and is a classic (*see pp18–19*).

Tarrafal

The main claims to fame for this fast-expanding port town stretching along a harbour bay in the southwest of the island are tuna fishing and canning, deep sea fishing for blue marlin, and the black volcanic sand on its beaches, believed to have medicinal properties.

Preguiça

A few rusty cannons define the hilltop fort that changed São Nicolau's fortunes when it was built to defend the sweeping bay of São Jorge. Two monuments within its low walls commemorate Pedro Alvares Cabral, who landed there in 1500 on a voyage of discovery to Brazil. The little fishing village below has a few bright houses and boats pulled up on the dark shingle shore. The little blue church dedicated to St Anthony is the centre of a big festival on 13 June every year.

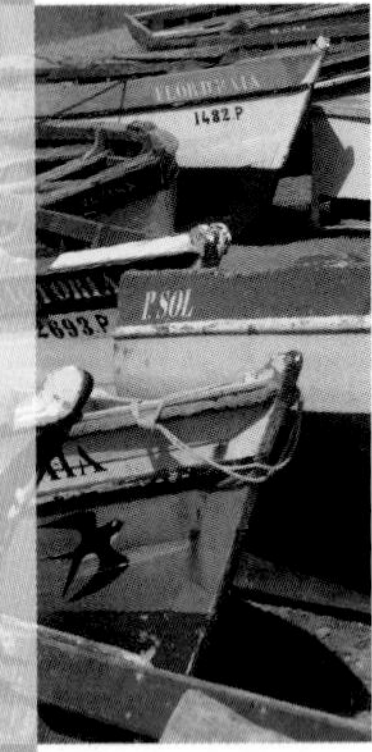

Drive: São Nicolau, over mountains to the sea

From pretty Ribeira Brava to the black sands of Tarrafal, via the lush green fields of Fajã, this is a spectacular drive.

See page 100 for map.

The drive is 52km (32 miles) for which you should allow a day to enjoy the varied scenery and perhaps take a walk in the National Park around Monte Gordo.

At the Shell petrol station end of town, take the Tarrafal road out past the police station and follow the signs to Carvoeiros.

1 Carvoeiros

There are great views along the coast as the road winds ever upwards. It zigzags above deep valleys, parched and brown with empty terraces, yet 25 years ago they were packed with banana plantations and the fruit exported to Portugal. Goats graze among scraggy trees where the sudden flurries of green indicate an underground water source. Returning emigrants are building smart clifftop houses overlooking the bay at Carvoeiros.

Take the valley road that winds down the hill past a cemetery to Queimadas. Craggy, cloud-wreathed mountains lie ahead.

2 Queimadas

Steep terraces surround this valley village where maize and beans grow among sweet potatoes and coconut palms. Between December and June, fields of sugar cane will be cut for the distilling of the *grogue* for which Queimadas has a good reputation.

Here you can see the two types of irrigation used on the island: the old Portuguese and Madeiran system of *levadas* (channels) and the new drip method. Drip irrigation is expensive initially, due to the amount of piping required, but as it delivers water directly to the root of each plant, it is much more efficient.

Queimadas means 'The Burning', a reference to the first inhabitants who, when they moved inland to escape pirate attacks, had to burn tracts of vegetation to build their houses and farms.

The road climbs steeply out of the valley to join the main route to Tarrafal. Continue to Fajã.

3 Fajã

It seems as if everything grows in hot and humid Fajã. Tomatoes, onions,

carrots and sweet potatoes, lush banana plantations, passion fruit, guava, mango and tall papaya trees all create an incredibly green experience. The irrigation that makes all this possible is due to a Mission de Coopération Françaises project, whose staff worked night and day between 1978 and 1983 to tunnel 2,800m (9,186ft) into the mountain and bring water to Fajã, where the people were living in poverty and waiting for rain.
Continue on the road to Tarrafal.

4 Dragon tree

Stop by the village water collection point for Lombo Pelado and get a close-up view of the prehistoric-looking Dragon tree (*Dracaena draco*) nearby. There are many more growing high in the mountains and they can be reached via a five-hour trek along a mule track, but this fine specimen is conveniently easy to admire. The water point is open for two hours twice a day, and you may see children filling big plastic containers and strapping them on to donkeys for the long walk home.
Continue along the road to Tarrafal.

5 Cachaço

There's a distinct chill in the air up at Cachaço, which is roughly the halfway point on the drive. Towering above it, Monte Gordo is São Nicolau's highest peak and a natural park protected zone. With the park's office in sight, but before you reach it, take a left turn to a little hilltop church, a place of pilgrimage on the last weekend in May, and affording a spectacular view down the valley to Ribeira Brava way below.
Rangers give guided walks on the mountain. You can get details about the park and its endemic plants by calling in at the office.

6 Tarrafal

After the dramatic mountain vistas and terraced greenery of the route so far, it's a bit of a shock to drive over the top of the next hill and find yourself in an entirely different environment. Sisal plants cling to crevices in sheer rock faces, binding sandy soil. Brown hills have wide, flat fields. At Cabeçalinho, new houses erected by American emigrants provide a stark contrast to the tiny traditional homes, which are built of stone and topped by a thatch of dried sugar-cane leaves smoothed down and tied like a parcel.

A wide asphalt road curves through a mountain-ringed dustbowl, and at the end of it is Tarrafal, a 100-year-old town that's developing fast. Fishing boats fill the harbour. Their main catch is tuna, which is canned in a nearby factory. Beneath red cliffs honeycombed with caves, brightly painted houses bring a splash of colour to the sweeping bay of black sand. A big tourist resort of apartments and boxy bungalows looks totally out of place along the coast.
Return by the same route to Ribeira Brava. Red rock glows in the evening light, low cloud envelops mountain peaks and the sheer drop into green valleys is beautiful.

Plants, trees and turtles

When the volcanic islands of the Cape Verde archipelago erupted from the sea millions of years ago, they were a blank canvas on which plant species, blown on the wind, dispersed by birds or carried by ocean currents, and animal species could attach themselves. Those that arrived and became established (indigenous species) had to adapt to the arid conditions and lack of rain. Over the millennia they have evolved and are today so different from their ancestors that they have to be considered a different species (endemic). About 80 of these endemic species, found nowhere else in the world, are known on the islands. A large number of them are on the endangered list.

Although probably never 'green' (the name Cape Verde refers to the green point on the coast of Senegal), in the early years of settlement there was certainly more natural vegetation than there is today. The number of towns named Tarrafal indicates that Tarrafe (*Tamarix senegalensis*) was abundant in the canyons near the coast. A large, strongly branched tree with tiny, feathery leaves, it grows on shallow sandy soils and can also be seen on shifting dunes. Similarly, there are many places called Figueira, after the Figueira-Brabo (*Ficus sycomorus* subspecies *gnaphalocarpa*), a species of fig that can grow to 20m (66ft)

Acacia trees in flower on Sal

Baby turtles in the waters off Sal

and is now so endangered that it is found only on steep, inaccessible escarpments. Espargos, the main town on Sal, got its name from Espargo (*Asparagus squarrosus*), a multi-branched creeping plant with spiny scale-like leaves that can cover vast areas. It is found in dry, rocky areas on the other islands, but no longer on Sal.

Used in the tanning of animal skins, Tortholho (*Euphorbia tuckeyana*) is a common component of scrub vegetation on rocky soils and Lorna (*Artemisia gorgonum*), a dense, aromatic shrub used in traditional medicine, is found in the less humid areas of Santo Antão, Santiago and Fogo.

There are several indigenous succulents to be seen, like the Gestiba (*Sarcostemma daltonii*) that drapes across big areas of rock. Its milky latex is widely used to treat tooth pain. Another succulent with medicinal uses is Salão (*Aeonium gorgoneum*), found on cliffs and escarpments and used to treat coughs and colds.

Looking strangely prehistoric with its spiky leaves grouped at the top of thick, strong branches, the Dragon tree (*Dracaena draco*) was once widespread but now only grows naturally on São Nicolau. Its 'blood' was once used for pain relief.

In an ongoing programme of reforestation, millions of trees have been planted in Cape Verde since independence, especially species of acacia. Although the indigenous Espinheiro-Branco (*Acacia albida*) is used, the South American species Acacia Americana (*Prosopis juliflora*) is most widespread.

The islands are one of the most important breeding sites for marine turtles in the world. They come ashore to lay their eggs and leave the resultant hatchlings to their own devices to make their way to the sea. Among turtle visitors to Cape Verde are the endangered Loggerhead (*Caretta caretta*) and Green turtle (*Chelonia mydas*), and the critically endangered Hawksbill (*Eretmochelys imbricato*) and Leatherback (*Dermochelys coriacea*). Conservation programmes are in place on all the 'turtle' islands.

Getting away from it all

From long walks on deserted, white sand beaches to hiking in high mountains and along lush valleys, even discovering birds found nowhere else in the world, the islands of Cape Verde offer endless opportunities for leaving the busy world behind. There are getaway locations everywhere on the archipelago, but two islands, Brava and Maio, stand out for their quiet isolation.

Brava

Tiny Brava is the most tropical and romantic of all the Cape Verde islands, famed for the flowers that fill its gardens, the trees that line its streets, its breathtaking mountain scenery and its old world charm. If reaching it was easy, it would quickly become a favourite destination. However, its airstrip closed years ago, buffeted by the powerful winds that churn the seas surrounding it and throw the already unreliable ferry schedules into disarray. Although only 20km (12½ miles) from neighbouring Fogo island, Brava feels very remote.

Sheer lava cliffs rise up from the seas, and it's a spectacular journey from the little port at Furna on a bumpy road of countless hairpin bends to Vila Nova Sintra. Named after Sintra in Portugal, this pretty little town with its old colonial houses sits in the crater of an extinct volcano, ringed by high mountains. Bougainvillea and hibiscus, almond trees, jacaranda and blue plumbago fill the gardens and line the streets. The mist and cloud that bring life to the plants can envelop the town for weeks.

Vila Nova Sintra was the home of the poet Eugénio Tavares, Cape Verde's most popular composer of *morna* songs. There's a plaque to his memory in the main square and his house can be seen at the top of the town. Steep paths from Nova Sintra take you into tiny villages clinging to mountainsides, *miradouras* (viewpoints) that on clear days afford spectacular views of terraced hills and the ocean, down remote valleys and up to Brava's highest point, the peak of Monte Fontaihas at 976m (3,200ft).

In one of Cape Verde's loveliest bays, the little fishing village of Fajã d'Água shelters under the mountains. Inland, there are surprises in tiny Sorno where carefully tended terraced fields stack up along the valley sides, fed by an ingenious collection of *levada* channels collecting water from a spring emerging from the mountain rock.

With an area of a mere 64sq km (25sq miles) and just 9km (5½ miles) at its widest point, Brava is the smallest of Cape Verde's inhabited islands. Seemingly hanging off the western end of the Sotavento (Leeward) islands, there's nothing but the roaring Atlantic to separate it from the next landmass, America. There's very little tourist infrastructure, but for the hiker with a sense of adventure, little Brava, 'the wild island', is very appealing.
Irregular ferry from São Filipe on Fogo to Furna.

Maio

For beach-lovers, sleepy Maio is a dream. Tourism is in its infancy, the friendliness of the islanders is legendary and there are so many beaches to laze and walk on that the most arduous task is deciding whether to stay on the one you're on or look for an even more deserted one. Lapped by an endless blue sea, some beaches hide below dunes and are invisible from the road. In summer, turtles emerge from the sea to lay their eggs on the empty beach at Morro.

Vila do Maio is hardly more than a large, neatly kept village of colourful houses edging a long beach where fishing boats land their catch. Its centrepiece is a big white 19th-century baroque church that rises above the spacious main square. An African-style hut with a conical roof, used by a local cooperative association, stands out among the mainly colonial British and Portuguese architecture. The old fort on the edge of town has been restored. Beyond the town lie some of the vast salt pans that occupied the British for nearly three centuries, when Vila do Maio was known as Porto Inglês.

The third of the flat sand and salt islands (Sal and Boavista lie to the north), Maio is the most easterly of the Sotavento (Leeward) islands, lying 25km (15½ miles) to the east of Santiago across a sea that can get very choppy. When its airport is open, it's a 15-minute hop from Praia. The barren but undulating landscape has some hills – Monte Penoso at 436m (1,430ft) being the highest – and the occasional oasis, but what really differentiates Maio from the other desert islands is the greenery created by the biggest acacia tree

Brava is known as the flower-filled island

Fishing boats on the beach at Vila de Maio

plantation on the archipelago, planted to restore Maio to its natural state.

One road has a circular route around the heart of this small, oval-shaped island of 268sq km (103sq miles) that at its longest stretches to 24km (15 miles). It links small villages and settlements and the *alugueres* (minibus taxis) that travel along it simply come and go when they're full. Time is not of the essence in Maio. An island of beautiful beaches, serene and unspoiled, it's simply a place to relax in peace.
Flights from Santiago. Three-hour ferry (on a rather ancient boat) from Praia, Santiago to Vila do Maio.

Rare birds

Some of the world's rarest birds can be found on Cape Verde, where up to 14 species are considered endemic to the islands. Most are found in isolated locations, some only on uninhabited islets where you'll need to engage the services of a local fisherman to get to see them.

With its high mountains and long, green valleys, Santiago is the richest island for endemic land birds. The world's last remaining nesting colony of Bourne's Heron is located deep in the Ribeira de Montanha. Many a Cape Verde Warbler can be spotted on hedges high in the hills at São Jorge dos Orgãos. The distinctive outline of the Grey-headed Kingfisher is a welcome sight on overhead wires and stone walls across many of the valleys and quite close to settlements. The Iago Sparrow and Cape Verde Swift also like the valley habitats. Rugged mountains harbour Cape Verde Buzzards, Cape Verde Falcons, Alexander's Kestrels and the Cape Verde race of the Rock Dove and Helmeted Guineafowl.

Ilhéu de Curral Velho on the island's southern tip and Ilhéu do Baluarte in the northeast, tiny islands off Boavista, are the only breeding sites of the Magnificent Frigatebird on the eastern side of the Atlantic. You'll need a good local driver to get you across the rocky and sandy terrain to the isolated spots on the coastline, where these superb birds can be seen soaring overhead and circling their breeding islets just offshore. They share these islets with large colonies of Brown Boobies.

The remote seabird islets of Razo and Branco, rising precipitously from the Atlantic, lie between São Nicolau and São Vicente and can be reached by boat from Tarrafal on the west coast of São Nicolau (*see p119*). Cape Verde Shearwaters abound here, an incredible sight when they glide home in the evening light. The entire world population of Razo Larks, numbering probably around 120, live on Razo island, where Ospreys breed and Redbilled Tropicbirds nest. There can hardly be a more exciting sight for the get-away-from-it-all birdwatcher.

Magnificent Frigatebirds breed off Santiago and Boavista

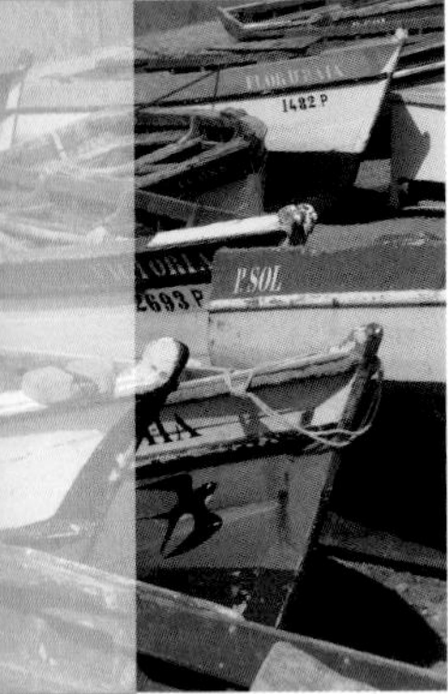

When to go

Cape Verde is sunny all year round, with day temperatures seldom dipping below 20°C (68°F) or rising above 30°C (86°F). Being in the North Atlantic off the west coast of Africa and trapped in the Sahel zone, rainfall on the islands is unpredictable, but ocean currents and the trade winds keep the climate moderate compared with that of the islands' neighbours on the same latitude.

In theory, Cape Verde's dry, tropical climate has two seasons: November to early July is the dry season; mid-July to October is the rainy season. However, as the country's history of devastating drought reveals, the rainy season doesn't always happen. In recent years, sporadic rains have fallen between September and December, but from year to year and island to island the rainfall is unpredictable.

The mountainous islands are at their most beautiful after the rains. September to December is usually the ideal time to visit Santiago, São Nicolau and Fogo. However, heavy rain can make the hiking trails of Santo Antão slippery, and low cloud tends to descend and block out the magnificent views.

Except in the very high mountains where winter temperatures can drop as low as 8°C (46°F), Cape Verde never really gets cold. Daily highs range from 20°C (68°F) in winter to around 30° (86°F) from July to October. There's a constant cooling breeze at the coast, which is welcome during the humid summer months but in the winter you'll need a light sweater in the evening. Fogo gets very hot and humid in the summer, and temperatures can reach 40°C (104°F) at Tarrafal on the coast of São Nicolau, but these are the extremes.

Sea temperatures fluctuate little, remaining between the low of 21°C (70°F) in February and March and the high of 25°C (77°F) in September and October. June to September is the best time for diving, and July to October for fishing.

Birdwatchers will find that March/ April is the start of the seabird breeding season, while October/November, when the vegetation should be at its peak on Santiago, is ideal for seeing breeding land birds. Every year from late May to September more than 3,000 Loggerhead turtles come ashore at Ervatoa beach on Boavista. Hotels and tour operators can arrange evening trips with a local driver to see them.

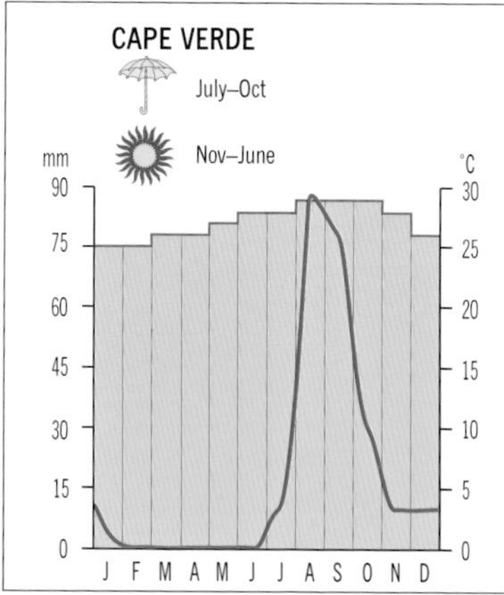

WEATHER CONVERSION CHART

25.4mm = 1 inch
°F = 1.8 × °C + 32

From January to June the hot Harmattan winds that blow from the Sahara can block out the sun, whip up the sand on the desert islands, and play havoc with inter-island flight schedules. But surfers love them. In January and February the waves are high at Ponta Preta on Sal. For Sal, Boavista and São Vicente, this is the peak time for windsurfing and kite surfing. There are gusts of up to 30 knots in Mindelo bay on São Vicente, where the average wind speed between January and June is 16 knots.

High and low season

November through to mid-December tends to be the cheapest time to visit Cape Verde. Hotel prices rise considerably over the Christmas period, also at Easter weekend, and again in Mindelo, São Vicente, for the Carnival (*see p20*). If you are planning on taking many inter-island flights, keep an eye on the dates of the big festivals, as planes get very full at those times. Resort hotels tend to keep prices quite high over the traditional European summer holiday months of July and August, which are the most popular with Italian visitors.

Most people travel to Cape Verde on the flight-and-accommodation holiday packages offered by tour operators, and there are not many opportunities for cheap flights. For independent travellers to the islands, scouring the websites of tour operators and airlines can sometimes prove fruitful.

Hiking in Santo Antão is best under the clear skies of the dry season

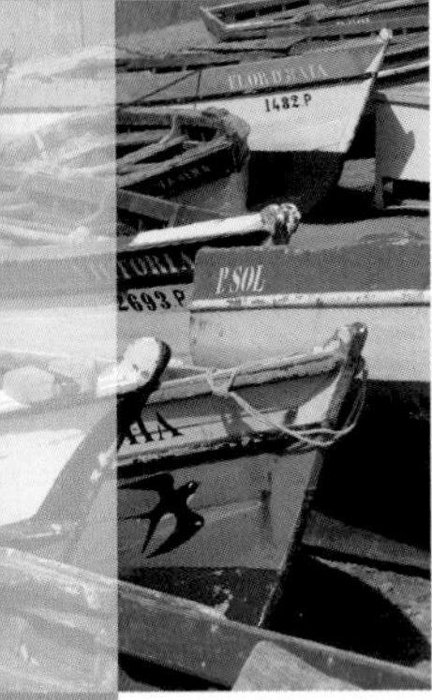

Getting around

The local mode of transport on all the islands is the aluguer, *which can take the form of a minibus or a pick-up truck with open-air benches at the back. There are buses serving the suburbs of Mindelo and Praia. Flights connect most of the islands, and ferries ply between some of them. Car hire is available on most of the islands, but it's preferable to hire a car complete with local driver.*

By air

The national airline, **Cabo Verde Airlines TACV**, connects most of the islands on schedules that range from several departures a day between the main hubs like Sal and Santiago, to two or three flights a week into smaller airports. Flights are not necessarily direct and may entail a stop at another island en route, which puts up the cost as each 'leg' is priced as a separate flight. One-way fares range from around 4,400 to 8,800CVE. The baggage allowance is 20kg (44lb).

There are certain essentials you need to pay heed to when flying within Cape Verde. First, book well in advance and check that the details on your ticket are correct. Flights can become very full and overbooked. Second, always reconfirm your flight 72 hours ahead. If your tickets have been arranged through your holiday company, the local representative should do this for you. Third, arrive at the airport in good time to get as near to the front of the check-in queue as you can.

Cancellations and delays happen for a variety of reasons, one being the weather conditions, especially in the windy months of January and February. Conditions may seem fine on the island you're leaving, but they may not be on the island you're trying to reach. Having said all that, TACV can be very good, on time and organised. However, it's just as well to be aware that not everything goes to schedule in Cape Verde.

Airports do not usually have any dedicated facilities for passengers with disabilities or buggy assistance.

Day-trip excursions from Sal to Boavista and Fogo are flown by charter airline **Cabo Verde Express.** The excursions can be booked through hotels and require a minimum of 17 passengers to operate.

By *aluguer*

If you don't mind being squashed into a minibus, or climbing up onto the open seating at the back of a pick-up truck, travelling by the ubiquitous *aluguer* is a great way to meet local people. It is best for short journeys and not suitable for people with disabilities.

Alugueres operate during the day, but not to timetables. They leave when they are full. Even then, someone in the front seat will still be shouting their destination to passers-by in the hope of piling in more fares. Expect the vehicles to be packed and noisy. Cape Verdeans love to chat and they discuss everything under the sun in high-speed Crioulo. Drivers favour loud reggae or local music.

The *alugueres* do run to a route, but have no 'bus stops'. Unless you are at their starting place, a central point in town that is likely to be obvious, you just flag one down along the road when you want to get on, and shout when you want to get off, which is when you pay, usually about 110CVE. Unlike the public transport in neighbouring West African countries, the vehicles are generally of recent manufacture and in very good condition. However, driving can be speedy and a little erratic.

On small islands, the *alugueres* run infrequently. Those used by people in outlying villages to get to their fields leave early in the morning, about 5am, and return around 1pm. Those that leave villages for town usually do so around 6am, returning between 11am and mid-afternoon. On Santo Antão, most but not all of the *alugueres* doing

A Cabo Verde Airlines inter-island aeroplane at Santiago airport

People boarding an *aluguer* in Ribeira Brava on São Nicolau

the mountain route between Porto Novo and Ribeira Grande are timed to coincide with ferry arrivals and departures. The cost is around 550CVE. Always check operating times. It's easy to get stranded, and chartering an *aluguer* is very expensive.

By bicycle

Cobbled roads, steep hills and the heat of the sun militate against cycling in Cape Verde. Set out with plenty of sunscreen and bottled water. Cycle hire is available through hotels on Sal and Boavista and on São Vicente at the Hotel Foya Branca near Mindelo.

By car

More car hire companies are opening up, but it's usually preferable to hire a taxi (*aluguer*) with a driver on the days you want to explore. The cobbled roads aren't easy, and on Sal and Boavista, where a four-wheel drive is essential if you are to get off the main road, it can be the most sensible option. Driving on sand and rocky terrain in total isolation sounds exciting, but if anything goes wrong, with no mobile phone signal and no 'passing' traffic, you could be in real danger.

It's becoming easier to find a driver who speaks English. A day's hire can be anything from 8,250CVE (a price often charged by hotels for a day's self-drive hire car) to 22,000CVE or more, depending on distances travelled. Driving is on the right, seatbelts must be worn and children under 12 must sit in the back seat.

By chartered fishing boat

When sea conditions are good, fishermen in Calhau on São Vicente can be persuaded to take you across to uninhabited Santa Luzia island and will charge about 5,500CVE for the return day trip. Fishing boats can also be hired to visit the seabird islets Raso and Branco off São Nicolau (*see p113*). Ask around at the harbour in Tarrafal.

By ferry

Ferries criss-cross between some of the islands, but they are extremely slow, have irregular timetables, can be very uncomfortable, and this method of travel is not recommended. There is one exception – the large car ferry operated by **Naviera Armas** that crosses between Mindelo and Santo Antão. It is reliable, leaves on time, arrives in under an hour, and the views of Mindelo harbour are stunning.

Buy your outgoing and return ticket at the office in front of the port gates. You need to be at the port, ticket in hand, half an hour before departure time. Suitcases and large hand luggage will be stored in a van for the crossing.

By organised tour

Excursions to the main sights are organised by hotels, tour agencies and tour operator representatives on all the islands. Half-day tours cost in the region of 4,400CVE.

By taxi

Both the saloon cars with 'taxi' signs found in towns and the public *alugueres* available for hire by individuals are known as 'taxis'. Agree the fare before you begin the journey. Most drivers are very honest and have a fixed rate but, as in all countries, there are exceptions. Tourists often get together to share the cost of hiring a minibus or *aluguer* taxi for a day's sightseeing. You are unlikely to find one with wheelchair facilities, but discuss your needs when booking. The taxi fare from Sal airport into Santa Maria is 1,100CVE, more at night. A tip is not expected.

A car ferry at Porto Novo on Santo Antão

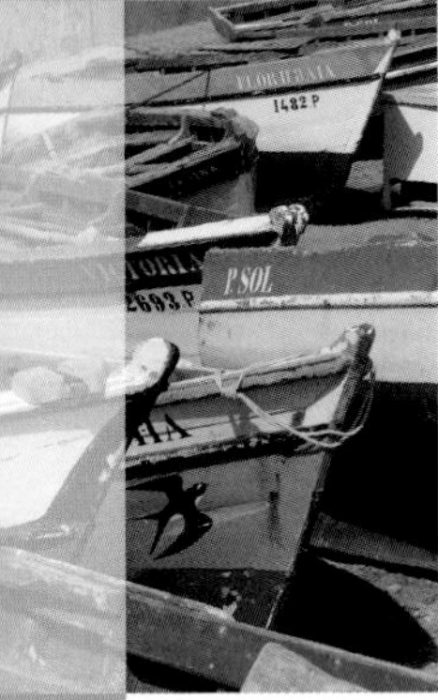

Accommodation

Sal has the biggest selection of hotels in Cape Verde, most of them facing onto the long, white sandy beach stretching out from the village of Santa Maria on the south coast. There are big complexes, much favoured by Italian visitors, along Boavista's superb Chaves beach, just a short drive from the airport. Santiago's international-standard hotels are in the country's capital, Praia. Smaller islands simply have guesthouses.

Cape Verde's foray into tourism began on Sal, the first island to have an international airport. Sal may be small, entirely desert and with few scenic attractions, but it has the white and fine-sanded beach that stretches along the south coast of the island. Lapped by a crystal-clear sea of incredible turquoise and sapphire blue, this is now lined with hotels. The accommodation ranges from a small hotel on a rocky promontory, where the courtyard rooms wrap around a small but pretty pool with ocean views and the restaurant is surrounded by the sea, to a huge complex with 1,000 rooms, like a small town encased by Moroccan-style walls and towers (*see pp148–9*). In between are a stylish hotel where you dine on the terrace under trees and several big all-inclusive properties featuring bungalow chalets in the gardens.

All the hotels have restaurants and bars, at least one swimming pool, offer a variety of water sports and feature brightly coloured flowers in their gardens. Air-conditioned en-suite rooms have satellite television with a limited number of channels in English, International Direct Dialling telephones and usually a hairdryer and fridge. All carry the local 4-star designation but, with the exception of the elegantly upgraded rooms at the Hotel Morabeza

The Morabeza Beach Club at Santa Maria on Sal's south coast

(*see p148*), generally equate more with the European 3-star rating.

Those in search of organised entertainment will find it here, especially in the Italian club hotels, but there are quiet options, too. Self-catering in well-appointed one- and two-bedroom apartments close to the beach is another alternative.

With the opening of Boavista's international airport, the building spree on the island has intensified. A gigantic, all-inclusive resort complex is rising on Chaves beach, minutes from the airport, built by a Spanish hotel chain. It will join the big Italian club hotel further along this 12km (7½-mile) long beach. Between them, a small hotel wreathed in bougainvillea has bungalow-style rooms where the sound of the sea lulls you to sleep.

Tourism in Cape Verde is closely linked with the beaches of the arid islands, but the spectacular, rugged mountain scenery of Santo Antão, Santiago, São Nicolau and the Fogo volcano attracts hikers and trekkers, for whom this little country sitting out in the Atlantic has been a well-guarded secret. Ecotourism is in its infancy, but two mountain retreats, Quinta da Montanha on Santiago (*see p156*) and Pedracin village on Santo Antão, are showing the possibilities of what could be done in the future. On Santo Antão several Europeans, mainly German, have opened up their homes to guests on long treks, or started small guesthouses by the sea at Ponta do Sol.

Bougainvillea flowering at Parque das Dunas Village on Chaves beach, Boavista

Fogo has one hotel of international standard, with an inviting pool and a good restaurant, and a selection of *pensões* (guesthouses) in pretty São Filipe town, while staying at the eco-guesthouse in the heart of the volcano crater is a unique experience (*see p157*). São Nicolau, still largely undiscovered, has a few clean and simple *pensãos* in Ribeira Brava.

There are no campsites in Cape Verde, and people with disabilities need to check very carefully with hotels before booking, as accessible facilities are limited.

Most accommodation is booked through tour operators, but the bigger hotels have websites with online booking facilities, and there are links to some smaller establishments on the website *www.caboverde.com*

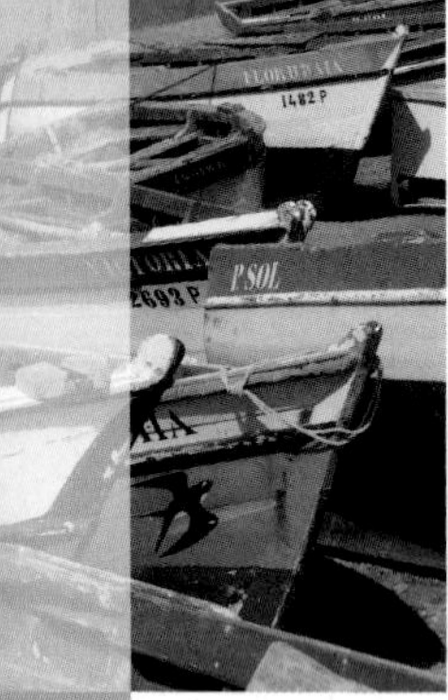

Food and drink

Fish, fresh from the sea, appears in all Cape Verde's restaurants, which are usually simple places, almost invariably spotlessly clean, serving up very generous helpings. The country's colonial history has resulted in a cuisine that's a mix of Portuguese, European and African influences. The traditional Crioulo dish of the islands is cachupa, *a hearty stew, and the local drink is* grogue, *distilled from sugar cane with a high alcohol content.*

Fish lovers will be in their element in Cape Verde. Tuna is landed daily, along with swordfish, wahoo, garoupa, sea bream, octopus, bica and a host of other local varieties caught from small boats by traditional methods. The lobster and prawns are excellent.

Mostly the fish is served grilled, when it is arguably at its best, and is accompanied by mixed salad, rice, vegetables and a plate of chips. Even the smallest of restaurants here present you with an array of dishes and generously sized meals.

Juicy steaks come from Brazil and South Africa, the source of most of the meat, fruit, salads and vegetables served in hotels. The many fruits and vegetables grown on Santo Antão, Fogo and Santiago find their way mainly into local markets.

Grilled chicken is also a popular menu staple. If you order it in a village or small town restaurant, you can be pretty sure it has lived locally and is free range.

Should the local fish restaurants pall, there are plenty of Italian restaurants to try. They offer some of the best pizzas and pasta you'll eat anywhere, possibly because many of the chef/owners have moved to Cape Verde from Italy.

Vegetarians will find their choices limited, particularly outside the hotels and main towns, but there will usually be omelettes, salad and pasta on the menu, or in more isolated places, a big plate of rice and beans.

The local speciality is *cachupa*. Cooked in every Cape Verdean home,

Freshly caught tuna on Sal

Bottles of *grogue* on display on Santo Antão

this is a hearty stew that takes a long time to prepare and is eaten for lunch, dinner and fried up for breakfast when it's topped with an egg and known as *cachupa guisada*. A legacy of the African slaves, when their owners gave them 'a bit of everything', it comes in two varieties. *Cachupa povera* (poor man's *cachupa*) is maize, beans, cassava, onions, sweet potato, cabbage and any other vegetable that is available. *Cachupa rica* (rich man's *cachupa*) has chicken, goat meat or tuna added to the mix. Many islanders consider that *cachupa* slow-cooked over a wood fire in a traditional pot is tastier than that cooked over gas.

Fresh goat's cheese is another island speciality and is served as a dessert accompanied by homemade mango, guava or papaya preserves. Maize, the staple food, is ground to made *xerém*, which looks rather similar to couscous.

Canja, a soup of chicken and rice, and *caldo de peixe* (fish soup) are served on special occasions.

The local beer is Strela, while the Portuguese Superbock and Sagres are also popular brands. But the real island drink is *grogue*. Made from pressed sugar cane and distilled everywhere, under a variety of conditions and in qualities that range from high to questionable, *grogue* has an alcohol content of around 45 per cent. It's the basis for *ponche* – *grogue* mixed with molasses made from the unfermented sugar-cane juice heated to form a thick syrup. For a real knockout, there's also *cortada*, a powerful mix of *grogue* and *ponche*.

Cape Verde also has its version of the Brazilian cocktail *caipirinha*, and is made here with *grogue*, squeezed lemon juice, ice and sugar. Wine from Fogo is also a must-try, as are the Fogo fruit liqueurs.

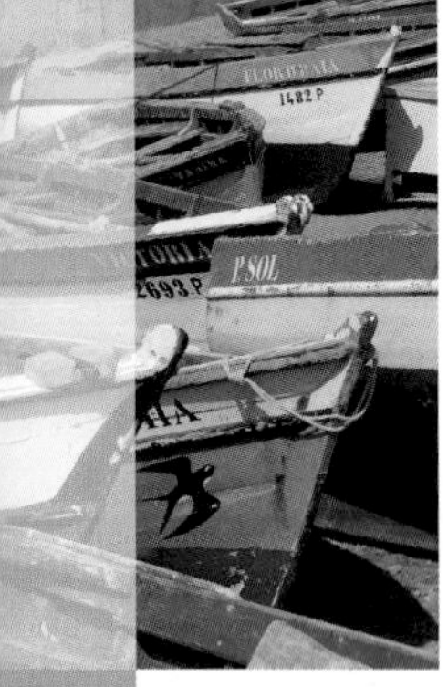

Entertainment

The islands are small and entertainment is limited, but when Cape Verdeans celebrate they know how to enjoy themselves to the full. From the many saints' day festivals to Carnival and the summer music festivals on Sal, Santiago and São Vicente, the partying goes on past sunrise. Visitors swept up in the action find themselves made very welcome. There's live music in bars and at weekends local nightclubs become lively after midnight.

Laidback Sal

Most of the entertainment on Sal happens in Santa Maria's hotels, especially in the all-inclusive resorts and Italian club hotels where the crew that have kept you active all day swing into evening action. Many hotel restaurants have a weekly Cape Verdean night, with big buffets showcasing local specialities and bands playing the distinctive sounds of the islands. They are open to non-residents. The Saturday evening Cape Verdean night on the terrace of the Hotel Morabeza (*see p148*) is a popular event.

The rustic Funaná restaurant right on the beach has live music every evening (*see pp149–50*). Go on one of their 'Roda Creola' nights, taste Cape Verdean dishes at the buffet, sip on a *caipirinha* or two and get in the mood for the lively *funaná* music played on traditional instruments and the mesmerising, sensual dancing that accompanies it.

Musicians play in some of the bars in Santa Maria village. The Pirata Disco at the entrance to the village has theme nights and is packed with locals at weekends, but only after 1am (*see p150*). A couple of hotels have discos, and you don't have to be a resident to get in.

Mid-September is when Sal lets its hair down with a two-night festival held on the beach. The music starts around 9pm and finishes roughly ten hours later (*see p21*).

Santa Maria's restaurants are small, and many surprise with the quality of their food. Service is usually charming,

Malaquias plays memorably at Nella's in Mindelo

A typical Cape Verde bar

but slow. In summer, when balmy nights follow humid days, eating outdoors is a pleasure. Café Cultura, edging the main square, is a popular choice (*see p149*). You'll need a sweater in winter, though, especially in windy January and February.

For all that Sal is the most developed island for tourism, there's not a lot happening at night. Fortunately, it has yet to take on the character of the Canary Islands 1,000km (620 miles) to the north. The closest you'll get is the Irish-run Tam Tam bar, which shows the big sporting events on a wide screen (*see p150*), and that's not very close at all.

Music in Mindelo, São Vicente

Mindelo on São Vicente is the musical heartbeat of Cape Verde. If you're looking for the best music, this is the place to be. From the wistful sounds of *morna* and the Latin beat of *funaná* in restaurants and bars to reggae, hip-hop and zouk in the pounding all-night clubs, Mindelo has it all.

Cesária Évora, Cape Verde's internationally renowned 'barefoot diva', and Bau, the brilliant guitarist, were both born in Mindelo and have homes there. Bau owns a music club and a member of his family has a small workshop where you can see exquisite stringed instruments being crafted by hand (*Aniceto Gomes Atelier de Violão, Monte Sossego, atrás de Cemitério. Tel: 238 914 623*). If he's doing a gig when you're there, don't miss it.

An evening at Nella's, a popular restaurant in the heart of town, is memorable for the food, the music and the atmosphere (*see p153*).

Carnival in Mindelo and the August music festival at Baía das Gatas (*see pp20–21*) are the big events on São Vicente's entertainment calendar.

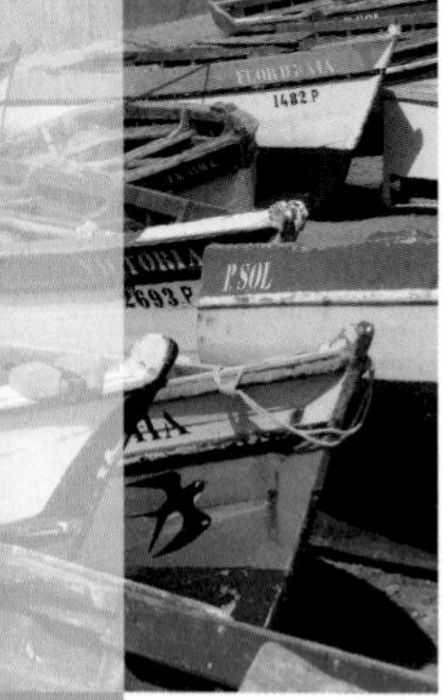

Shopping

Cape Verde is not a country where you are likely to seriously dent your bank balance, or attract the eye of an airport customs officer after an expensive shopping spree. Small souvenirs of your holiday are the usual offerings, and while Senegalese traders may insist their African carvings are Cape Verdean, the selection of true island crafts is not large.

Mindelo on São Vicente is the best place to see and buy crafts. The **Arte Crioula** shop (*corner of the Praça Nova*) displays items from all the islands under one roof. Here you'll find hand-embroidered cloths, tableware, ceramics, batik T-shirts and tops, woven baskets, handbags fashioned from pieces of polished coconut shell, little lava stone houses, clay figures, dolls, woven wall hangings and imaginative toys crafted from wire and recycled cans.

At the other end of the Praça, the **Atelier Joana Pinto** (*Rua de Sénégal*) is where Joana designs and makes colourful batiks and where her stunning wall-hangings are woven by hand using a traditional loom. The powerful images reflecting Cape Verdean life and the strong clear colours are very striking.

The **Mindelo Cultural Centre**, in the 19th-century Customs House facing the sea, has a small shop selling island crafts. The **Galeria Alternativa** (*Rua do 5 de Julho*) is also worth investigating.

On Santiago, traditional crafts are being revived in São Domingos. Clay potters and weavers of *pano de terra* (traditional cloth) work behind **Centro Artesanatos**, a shop selling the finished

Crafts for sale in Mindelo, São Vicente

products, which is on the main road and a popular stop on excursions. The naïve paintings by young Rabelados (*see pp88–9*) make unusual souvenirs. If you don't get to their settlement, you'll find a selection in the information centre at the fort above Cidade Velha.

On the Plâto in Praia, take a look at the Palácio da Cultura on the main square and the craft shop near the market (*Avenida Amílcar Cabral*). Santiago's lively music tradition means there are several places to buy CDs. **Quintal da Música**, a popular bar with live music in the evenings, is one of them (*Avenida Amílcar Cabral*).

Behind the church on the main square in Sal Rei on Boavista, **A Baleia Azul** is a lovely little gift shop selling handcrafted bead and shell jewellery.

Buy *grogue* on Santo Antão and Fogo wine and liqueurs at the Cooperativa in the volcano crater. Santo Antão is also good for mango and papaya jams and preserves. If you don't get to these islands, you'll find the products on the shelves of the various mini-markets in Santa Maria, Sal.

Sal, naturally, has the most souvenir shops. They are dotted among the bars and restaurants on the main street, or well signposted if on a side street. Here you can buy sarongs, bikinis, beachwear and surf gear – although being imported they are expensive – and plenty of T-shirts with island messages and innumerable African curios, paintings and woodcarvings. Some of these are carved in side-street workshops by the immigrant West Africans who do their utmost to get you into the shop, where bartering is acceptable.

A vase made in Santa Maria, Sal

To find Cape Verdean-made crafts go to the **Centro d'Artisanato** (*Rua 1 de Junho*). The whirr of sewing machines in the back tells you where the colourful clothes are made and local people string beads and carve souvenirs from stone. Further along Rua 1 de Junho, the **Oficina d'Arte** pottery produces attractive European-style ceramics, especially vases. The shop also sells brightly coloured shirts, blouses, shorts and bead jewellery. Nearby, **Sol e Sal** is great for gifts, including neat little sachets of Sal salt, bicycles, motorbikes and trucks made from recycled cans, and necklaces and art. It's usually open in the evenings.

Hiking in Cape Verde

The contrasting islands of Cape Verde delight walkers of every ability. The views from the mountains and through lush *ribeiras* (valleys) are spectacular and hiking on the slopes of Fogo's volcano is an experience few other countries can match.

Most of the hiking trails are on cobbled paths constructed from local stone and laid by hand. Some are so steep and lead seemingly nowhere, but are in daily use to reach tiny, isolated villages teetering on rock faces or near-vertical, neatly terraced fields. Others meander along lower slopes, past cattle farms and plantations of bananas and sugar cane.

Santo Antão's mountains make challenging hiking, but the views are unbeatable

Even the flat islands have their potential, especially for those who prefer not to tackle steep ascents and descents. Boavista's sinuous dunes and its endless, almost deserted, white-sanded beaches are perfect for long walks. In the late afternoon and evening when the sun is low and warm light patterns the lapping surf, long-legged wading birds tiptoe in the shallows. On Sal, just walk to the end of Santa Maria village and you find low sandy ridges patterned with grasses and hardy succulents on a coastline few people bother to explore.

Serious hikers head for Santo Antão, where the towering mountains are challenging and the rewards are huge. But just walking for a while along a fairly flat *ribeira* brings you in contact with local people and wherever you look the views are stunning.

You can walk for miles on Boavista's deserted beaches

Alugueres traverse the main roads out of Vila de Ribeira Grande. One popular 10-km (6-mile) hiking route entails taking this form of transport up the Porto Novo road to Água das Caldeiras, then making the steep descent from pine forests through Ribeira da Torre to the sea. The route encompasses vistas of craggy mountains and jagged rocks, isolated villages – one of them on a ledge just wide enough to take a row of tiny houses and a footpath – tiny, seemingly inaccessible terraces and the sweeping green of cultivated fields.

As an alternative to the *ribeiras*, there's a good 12-km (7½-mile) coastal route that will take you from Ponta do Sol to two dramatically poised villages. The first is Fontainhas, reached by a winding cobbled road that follows the mountain folds. Perched atop a knife-edge rock above a deep valley, it seems to have stepped out of the pages of a storybook. The second is Chã de Igreja, a pretty village of bright little houses built on an outcrop. Between them lie views of terraced *ribeiras*, tiny villages and the long, indented coastline from a road hacked out of the mountain rock.

Wherever you are walking, always carry water and an adequate supply of food, and wear sunscreen and a hat. On long hikes, especially in the mountains, it is advisable to hire a guide.

Never set out into the mountains without taking advice from local people. They understand the vagaries of the weather and the swirling mists, and also which routes are slippery or should not be attempted after rain. In the winter months, between December and February, the higher reaches and cloud-piercing peaks of Santo Antão can be cold, with temperatures sometimes dropping as low as 6°C (43°F).

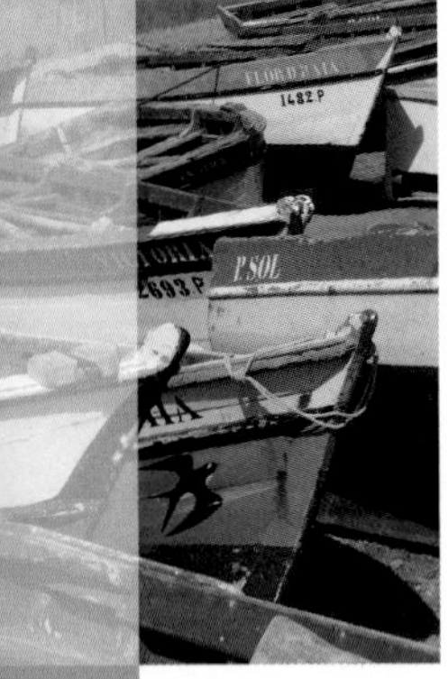

Sport and leisure

It's the great beaches and year-round sunshine that draw many visitors to the archipelago. Sal is the centre for water sports, especially windsurfing, kite surfing and scuba-diving, as well as fishing for tuna, wahoo and blue marlin. But Cape Verde is a superb hiking destination, too, with the mountains and lush valleys of Santo Antão, Santiago and São Nicolau affording spectacular views, while climbing Fogo's volcano is a unique experience.

Big game fishing

Clear water, ocean currents and a lack of commercial fishing all contribute to the abundance of fish found in Cape Verde waters. The big catches are yellowfin tuna, dorado, wahoo, amberjack, kingfish and sailfish. All are plentiful close offshore. Blue marlin is also found here from around June to October. However, the best marlin run is south of São Nicolau and in the channel between São Vicente and Santo Antão. Boats from these islands are based in Mindelo, São Vicente and Tarrafal on São Nicolau. Ask around at the harbour in Tarrafal or book through **Agência Santos & Santos** in Ribeira Brava (*Estância Baixo. Tel: 235 1830*). Game fishing is also available from Sal (*see p151*).

You can book half-day and full-day fishing trips, with trolling, bottom fishing, surf casting, rock fishing and spinning all available. It's as well to pre-book before you arrive as Cape Verde is becoming well known among sport fishing aficionados from all over the world.

Boat trips

The yellow 'submarine' *Neptunus* is a familiar sight anchored in the bay near Santa Maria's jetty (*see p151*). All kinds of fish can be seen from its underwater viewing chamber and if you are lucky you may see dolphins leaping and diving off the coast. *Neptunus* visits two wrecks. To the west of the beach, shoals of silver grey- and black-striped fish, slim trumpet fish and colourful parrotfish circle around the old boiler of the *Bolama*, a Portuguese cargo-carrying steamship that sank during a storm in 1920. On night excursions, lobsters can be seen emerging from their hiding holes. East of Santa Maria, the *Santo Antão*, an inter-island cargo and passenger ship that sank in 1965, lies broken into three parts on the sandy bottom, providing habitation for numerous kinds of fish. It's possible to see stingrays there.

You can go on a half-day boat trip along Sal's coast with time for swimming and possibly snorkelling.

Book through your hotel or at the jetty. Barracuda Tours (*see p150*) also arrange island boat trips. You can also take a day excursion from Sal to Boavista. The *Ilan Voyager* is a high-speed trimaran that does the crossing between Palmeira on Sal and Sal Rei on Boavista in 90 minutes.

Diving

With its caves, reefs, canyons and shipwrecks all abounding in fish, Sal is the ideal island for diving (*see pp134–5*). Summer, between April and November, is the best season but dives can be experienced all year round. Big fish come relatively close to shore. Whales can be seen between March and May, whale sharks and manta rays between July and November. The turtle season is June to October.

In this tropical underwater world are shoals of sea bream, perch, horse mackerel, tuna and grouper, and fish with intriguing names like bastard and pigsnout grunt, bulldog dentex and Monrovia doctorfish. You can dive among colourful Guinean parrotfish, blue-spotted triggerfish, red-and-white scorpion fish and grey snapper, which is red. The moray eel is found in Cape Verde waters and there are some unusual corals and underwater flora to be discovered.

There are 16 dive sites off Sal, all reachable on short boat trips from Santa Maria. They include cliffs and pinnacles and a 300m (985ft) undersea

A good day's fishing off Sal

Quad bikers in the dunes near Santa Maria on Sal

'mountain' visited by tuna fish, marlin, mantas, stingrays and whale sharks. The easy '3 Grutas' dive reveals lobsters, turtles and every kind of tropical fish, while the wreck of a Russian ship that sank in 2006 has become an artificial reef that schools of soldier fish, frogfish, trumpet fish and jack fish call home, along with crustaceans such as lobster and cuttlefish.

If you want to learn to dive, Cabo Verde Diving (*see pp150–51*) organises PADI (Professional Association of Diving Instructors) courses at all levels and its multilingual team is very experienced in working with beginners. The introductory PADI Discover Scuba Diving course can be done in about four hours, two hours in the morning, two in the afternoon, not necessarily on the same day.

Quad biking

Small group excursions by Motoquad, Funquad and Buggy across low dunes and endless sand can be booked through hotels on both Sal and Boavista. (*See pp151 & 152–3) for operators.*)

Trekking and hiking

The rugged mountains and deep *ribeiras* (valleys) of Santo Antão and the slopes and valleys of Santiago and São Nicolau are stunningly beautiful places to walk, and the volcano crater of Fogo is fascinating. Day walks or trekking holidays can be booked through tour operators, and many hotels can also arrange hiking trips. Day walks usually include transport to the starting point, a packed lunch and pick-up by *aluguer* (minibus taxi) at

Ponta Preta on Sal has ideal waves for windsurfing

the end of the route to return to your accommodation.

Turtle watching

Marine turtles come ashore to lay their eggs on Sal's east and west coast beaches in summer, but the best island to see them is Boavista. This is one of the largest breeding grounds in the world for Loggerhead, Green, Leatherback and Hawksbill turtles.

From May to September, more than 3,000 Loggerhead turtles (*Caretta caretta*) come ashore at night to find a suitable site to lay around 40 golf ball-sized eggs and then return to the ocean. When the hatchlings emerge, the beach becomes a sea of scuttling brown.

Ervatoa beach on the east coast of Boavista is the main nesting site and hotels can arrange trips to it. A conservation group, Natura 2000, has a project at Ervatoa to track turtles and protect the habitat. There is concern locally that the rise in tourism to this sparsely populated island could affect the turtle breeding. It's important not to get too close to them, shine lights on them or disturb their eggs.

Windsurfing and kite surfing

The conditions are so good for windsurfing on Sal that international teams train there during the winter and championships are also held there. Ponta Preta has the famous big waves. Water temperatures of at least 21°C (70°F) add to the pleasure of water sports in Cape Verde, and there's plenty of quality equipment available for rental.

At Santa Maria the wind is a steady Force 4/5 along the beach. Summer, when the wind slackens, is better for beginners. Surf Zone alongside the Morabeza Beach Club (*see p151*) has introductory courses in both windsurfing and kite surfing. On average, it takes three to four hours of instruction in windsurfing before you can practise on your own; six to ten hours to learn the sport of kite surfing.

Other good beaches on Sal are at Canoa in Murdeira Bay, which is considered an easy and safe spot, and Salinas, which has no dangerous currents. Boavista is also a popular island for windsurfing.

A kite surfer enjoying Sal's waves

Diving off the coast of Sal

Rocky ridges, pinnacles and boulders, great arches and deep caves, sheer cliffs and fissures filled with tropical and Mediterranean fish: the beauty of Sal lies beneath the sea. Here the Atlantic Ocean flows from shades of limpid turquoise to deepest emerald and sapphire. Within it live species of fish found nowhere else in the world.

Cape Verde's marine life is quite different from that of its nearest neighbours, the Canary Islands 1,000km (620 miles) to the north and the colder waters of Senegal about 450km (280 miles) to the east, which makes it a fascinating place to dive. The island of Sal has the most accessible sites, many within a short boat trip from the dive centres at Santa Maria.

With sea temperatures around 24°C (75°F), the diving season is year round, but it's at its best during the summer months of April to November. The hot Harmattan winds blowing from the Sahara in winter bring the swells that delight kite- and windsurfers, yet there are still sites that provide natural shelter.

Catfish, slipper lobsters and the moray eels that are endemic to Cape Verde emerge from the ledges and crevices of wide caves on Sal's northwest coast. In summer, this is the place for the classic view of divers swimming through a beam of light, and surfacing through Buracona's 'blue eye' (*see pp35 & 37*).

Tropical fish haunt volcanic rock fissures in the far north. On the west coast the labyrinth of caverns at Regona is home to crustaceans and nurse sharks. Caves surrounded by yellow coral, huge rocks where giant shoals of fish congregate, and endemic and rare species all lie off Sal's southwest coast.

In the southern bay around Santa Maria, moray eels, big crabs and multi-hued lobsters crowd the small caves and rock wall at Pontinha. The dive site at Cavala descends to 65m (213ft) and offers encounters with every kind of pelagic fish, including amberjacks, guelly jacks and snappers.

There's easy diving at Très Grutas (Three Caves), home to lobsters,

Divers looking at fish off Sal

turtles and myriad tropical fish. All Cape Verde's endemic species are found at Farol, where sand surrounds the rocky platforms and the dive depths range from 6–18m (20–59ft).

Then there are the wrecks. *Kwarcit*, a Russian fishing trawler known locally as 'Boris', is upright and still intact. Covered in sponges and corals, it is full of fish, including silver sea bream, various blennies and gobies, pufferfish, wrasses and colourful parrotfish. Stingrays loiter in the sand beneath the bow. Visiting fish include dorado (dolphin fish), grouper and jacks. Big stingrays favour the wreck of the *S Antão* where endemic Guinea grunts, lizardfish, puffer and trumpet fishes are found among nudibranch corals and soapfish.

East of Santa Maria, bright yellow polyps cover the big overhangs of the ridge at Choclassa where parrotfish, surgeonfish, goatfish, Atlantic bigeyes and scribbled filefish gather in large numbers. Dives at varying depths from 20–40m (66–131ft) on this site allow for sightings of moray eels, lobsters, turtles, stingray, tuna, marlin and various mantas. Nurse sharks slip through the sand at around 26m (85ft). Other sharks in these waters include hammerheads, lemons and sand tigers. Humpback and whale sharks arrive in summer.

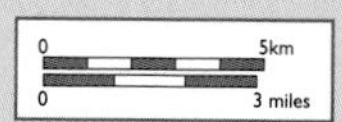

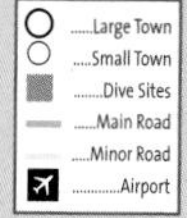

Children

With their many sports facilities and organised activities, children's clubs and pools, the all-inclusive hotel club resorts of Sal are well geared for family holidays. As much as Cape Verdeans love children, you will not find anything especially for them elsewhere. The most developed islands for family tourism are Sal and Boavista.

Big, all-inclusive club hotels stretch out along the wide beach at Santa Maria on Sal. They organise activities throughout the day and entertainment at night, offer several restaurants and have either a separate baby and children's club with its own pool, or big pools that include a children's section. Windsurfing, kite surfing, beach volleyball, body boards, tennis, archery and table tennis are among the activities on offer.

Most of these hotels are Italian-owned and attract an Italian clientele, while the massive Riu complex at the end of the bay has groups from continental Europe, mainly Germany. So while your children will be entertained, it may not be in English.

Children, such as these here on Boavista, play happily in the streets

The beaches are all soft sand and the water is clear, warm and inviting, but it isn't always safe to swim in the sea. The waves can be strong and there are no lifeguards. Local children splash around in the shallows and practise body surfing.

Of the excursions available on Sal, older children will enjoy seeing the mirage at Terra Boa, and going on the *Neptunus* 'submarine', which has an underwater viewing chamber. Sailing boat trips offer the potential of swimming and snorkelling off the coast.

The Sal Turtle Action Group started turtle-watching excursions during the months when Loggerhead turtles come ashore to lay their eggs on western and eastern beaches. Ask at your hotel if there are any trips if you are there between May and September.

Kids will love the beaches at Santa Maria on Sal

Self-catering

Renting an apartment can be a good option for families. Well equipped, with air conditioning, cooking facilities and (usually) satellite television, they have a patio or balcony and are often set around a pool in landscaped gardens. (Bookings can be made through: *www.holidaylets.net; www.ownersdirect.co.uk; www.holiday-rentals.co.uk*).

You'll probably find you are eating out a lot. The few mini-markets sell basics, but the selection is very limited. A 60 per cent tax makes anything imported expensive. There's a good bakery in Santa Maria village where you can buy breakfast supplies (*Padaria Dâdo, Rua 1 Julho*). Women selling fruit and vegetables often gather on the roadside nearby. And if you want fish, just stroll along to the pier when the fishermen come in with their catch around midday. For any child that thinks fish comes in fingers, this will be a revelation.

Bring all the baby things you need, including nappies. They are imported, so are very expensive and supply is limited. Also bring sunblock, which is essential, and a first-aid kit. There's a small pharmacy in the village that may be able to help if you have a problem. Pack reading material, iPod, games and everything you think you'll need to keep young minds occupied.

Cape Verdeans are crazy about football. They know all the England teams and big name players, even if they don't speak English. The small sports stadium in Santa Maria village, opposite the Tam Tam bar (*see p150*), is always in use and the kids there would welcome a visiting player.

For Cape Verdeans, eating out in restaurants and hotels is reserved for special occasions and celebrations. It's a real family affair with all the children included. Your children will be welcomed in restaurants and there may be a children's menu. There are lots of good pizza places in Santa Maria, too.

Essentials

Arriving and departing

By air

Astraeus Flystar has scheduled flights from London Gatwick and Manchester to Sal and Boavista. Cape Verde's national airline TACV flies from London Stansted to Sal and Santiago, and from Amsterdam, Bergamo, Lisbon, Munich, Paris, Porto, Warsaw, Banjul (Gambia), Bissau (Guinea-Bissau), Dakar (Senegal), Freetown (Sierra Leone), Fortaleza (Brazil) and Boston (USA) to either Sal or Santiago. TUI (Thomsonfly) flies from London Gatwick and Manchester. TAP Air Portugal flies from Lisbon to Sal and Santiago. Condor Air flies from Frankfurt to Sal. There are also charter flights from Italy, Portugal and Germany.

Sal's **Amílcar Cabral International Airport (SID)** (*Tel: 241 1394*) is 20km (12 miles) from Santa Maria along a good asphalt road and 2km (1¼ miles) from the island's main town Espargos. Taxis leave from outside the arrivals terminal and the 20-minute journey from the airport to Santa Maria costs around 1,100CVE, more at night.

The airport has one terminal and is not large, but has been upgraded. Facilities include foreign currency exchange, some small shops, Internet access, two cafés and a duty-free shop.

Boavista International Airport (BVC) began operating in November 2007 and has up-to-date facilities (*Rabil, about 3km/1¾ miles from Sal*

Amílcar Cabral International Airport on Sal

Rei; tel: 251 1070). Santiago's **Praia International Airport (RAI)** is quite spacious, has a café in the departure area, currency exchange and ATM (cash machine) (*about 2km/1¼ miles from city centre; tel: 263 1010*). An international airport at Mindelo, São Vicente, is scheduled for completion during 2008.

Departure tax is included in the air ticket. A departure form has to be completed. At Sal airport you can collect one at the entrance to the check-in desk hall. Sal has a duty-free shop and a small café with an outside seating area after passport control.

By sea

Some cruise ships include Mindelo on their cruise itineraries.

Customs

You are allowed to import free of tax 200 cigarettes, 1 litre of spirits and a reasonable amount of perfume in opened bottles.

Electricity

The electricity supply on Cape Verde is 220V 50Hz. The standard European two-pin plug is used. If you need an adaptor, be sure to take one with you. Electricity supply can be patchy, but hotels have generators.

Internet

More and more Internet cafés are opening, and you shouldn't have much trouble finding one in the main towns of the islands. Hotels have Internet facilities for guests' use, but they tend to be more expensive. Connection can be quite fast, but is patchy. Don't expect Wi-Fi hotspots.

Money

The currency is the Cape Verde escudo, signed as CVE or $ placed at the end of the amount. It can only be purchased in Cape Verde. Aim to spend all your local currency while you're there, as it cannot be reconverted. Notes are in denominations of 5,000, 2,000, 1,000 and 500CVE. Coins are in denominations of 200, 100, 50, 20, 10, 5 and 1CVE.

The CVE is pegged to the euro, with an official fixed exchange rate of 110CVE to €1. In practice, it can vary a little and some hotels appear to set their own rate. Euros can be used on Sal, and also in Praia and Mindelo, but are not widely accepted across all the islands. When paying in euros you will find they are taken as the equivalent of 100CVE.

Traveller's cheques in sterling or euros can be cashed at banks (expect long queues and waiting times) and some hotels. However, they are very difficult to cash outside tourist areas. Check the fee you will be charged to cash them, as it can be very high.

ATMs (cashpoint machines) outside banks in the main towns dispense escudos. Visa cards are the most widely accepted by these machines. At banks,

The view from Quinta da Montanha on Santiago

currency can be obtained from credit cards (mainly Visa and MasterCard) but the charges are very high. Hotels will exchange the main hard currencies at reception, where the day's rates are on display.

Cape Verde is very much a cash economy and where credit cards are accepted for payment there will be a significant charge for their use, usually between 5 and 6 per cent.

Opening hours

Everything closes on Sundays and public holidays. Shops close at lunchtime on Saturday for the weekend. Banking hours are Monday to Friday 8am to 3pm.

Shopping hours are Monday to Friday 8am or 8.30am to noon or 12.30pm, reopening at 2pm or 2.30pm until 6pm to 6.30pm. Some shops are shut in the afternoons. In Santa Maria on Sal, the closing time is usually 7pm, while many souvenir shops stay open until late in the evening.

Passports and visas

Visitors of all nationalities require a visa to enter Cape Verde. Your passport must be valid for six months after your arrival there. Visas can only be obtained from countries where there is a Cape Verde embassy, but the UK and Ireland are not among them. Several UK tour operators specialising in Cape Verde organise the visa for their clients. The cost is either included in the price of your holiday, or an extra charge. The information will be in the computer at the immigration desks, making your entry into the country a smooth one.

If you do not have a pre-arranged visa, one can be issued on arrival, prior to passing through immigration. Expect a long wait while it is processed. The cost is around 45€, payable in cash, although it can fluctuate. (It can be paid in other currencies.)

In continental Europe there are Cape Verde embassies in Paris, Brussels, Berlin, Rome, The Hague, Lisbon and Luxembourg. Cape Verde's Ambassador to the UK is based in Brussels (*Ambassade du Cap-Vert, Avenue Jeanne 29, 1000 Bruxelles. Tel: (+32) 2 64 69 025. Email: emb.caboverde@skynet.be*).

In the USA, the embassy in Washington, DC also deals with enquiries from Canada (*Embassy of the*

Republic of Cape Verde, 3415 Massachusetts Avenue, NW, Washington, DC 20007. Tel: (202) 965 6820. www.virtualcapeverde.net).

The Embassy for Southern Africa is in Angola (*Embassy of the Republic of Cape Verde, Rua Oliveira Martins No 3, Luanda, Angola. Tel: (+244-2) 321765, 3210412. Email: embaicv.ang@snct.co.ao*).

Cape Verde is not represented in Australia or New Zealand.

Pharmacies

There are reasonably well-stocked pharmacies in all the main towns but you should take your prescription medicine requirements with you. There are no 24-hour pharmacies. (*Open: Mon–Fri 8am–noon & 3.30–7pm; in larger towns also: Sat 8am–noon.*)

Sal

Farmácia Rama, Entrada, Santa Maria. Tel: 242 1340.

Santiago

Most districts of Praia have a pharmacy. Farmácia Africana is on the Plateau.
Farmácia Africana, Avenida Amílcar Cabral. Tel: 261 2776.

Santo Antão

Farmácia São João Baptista, Vila Porto Novo. Tel: 222 2348.

São Nicolau

Farmácia Gabi, Ribeira Brava. Tel: 235 1173.

São Vicente

There are several pharmacies in Mindelo but the Farmácia Jouem is one that stays open during the lunch hours.
Farmácia Jouem, Avenida 12 de Setembro, Mindelo. Tel: 232 4530.

Post

Every main town has a post office and usually it's a modern, well-equipped building with a variety of services. You can make phone calls, send faxes and arrange money transfers as well as buy stamps and post mail.

Public holidays

1 January	New Year's Day
20 January	Heroes' Day
February/March/April	Carnival and Good Friday
1 May	Labour Day
5 July	Independence Day
15 August	*Nossa Senhora da Graça* (Day of Our Lady of Grace)
12 September	National Day
1 November	All Saints' Day
25 December	Christmas Day

Municipal days

Each island honours the saint on whose day the island was discovered, or its patron saint, with a public holiday.

17 January	Santo Antão
22 January	São Vicente
30 April	Fogo (São Filipe)
3 May	Maio (Santa Cruz)
24 June	Brava (São João)

4 July	Boavista (Santa Isabel)
15 August	Santiago's main Municipal Day (*Nossa Senhora da Graça*), but Tarrafal municipality has a public holiday on 15 January and the Santa Catarina area on 25 November
15 September	Sal (*Nossa Senhora das Dores*)
6 December	São Nicolau

Festivals

Every island has an array of saint's day festivals celebrated in various towns. Those lasting several days include the big carnivals in Mindelo (São Vicente) and Ribeira Brava (São Nicolau) in February/March, Fogo's Bandeira de São Filipe at the end of April, Brava's Festa de São João in June, Santo Antão's São João Baptista in June, and Santiago's *Tabanka* processions in June and July (*see p63*). Most islands celebrate the Feast of Santa Cruz on 3 May, São João on 24 June and São Pedro on 29 June.

Suggested reading and media

Books

Most of the books about Cape Verde are in Portuguese and some have been translated into French or Italian. Novels and poetry by Cape Verdean writers, in Portuguese or Crioulo, have yet to be translated into English.

If you can find them, the following two books are worth reading for background information on the history of Cape Verde.

The Fortunate Isles by Basil Davidson (Hutchinson, 1989), subtitled 'A Study in African Transformation', covers the liberation struggle and the challenges of the post-independence years.

Antonio's Island by Marcelo Gomes (Braiswick, 2002), subtitled 'Missing pages of History for Blacks and Hispanics', is by an American author with Cape Verdean ancestry.

For information on the birds of Cape Verde, read: *The Birds of the Cape Verde Islands* by Cornelis Hazevoet (British Ornithologists' Union, 1995).

Media

There are no English newspapers in Cape Verde. For island news, look at the website of the weekly *A Semana*, which has an English section (*www.asemana.cv*). The local television channel TNCV sometimes shows films in English. Satellite television is widespread, with Portuguese, Italian, German and French stations predominating in hotels, where you seldom get more than one channel in English, either CNN or BBC World. Cape Verdeans are passionate about sport and Brazilian soap operas.

Tax

The standard rate of VAT in Cape Verde is 15 per cent. VAT at 6 per cent is levied on restaurant prices.

Telephones

The international dialling code for Cape Verde is 238. International calls from both landline and mobile phones are very expensive. The cost of calls made from hotels can be eye-watering. In Santa Maria, the kiosk on the main square has facilities for lower cost calls and some Internet cafés also offer cut-rate phone calls. Try 3D.Com, deep in the heart of the village in Santa Maria, which also rents out DVDs. There are public phone boxes at CV Telecom centres and Post Offices, where you can buy a phone card for around CVE770.

Mobile phone reception is improving but can be patchy on some islands, and the mobile you've brought with you may or may not work depending on your service provider. If you get your phone unlocked before you travel, you can buy a CV Telecom SIM card, which costs 2,000CVE and includes some credit; they are available at CV Telecom centres. A call from a mobile to the UK will then cost about 110CVE per minute.

A pretty *pensão* in Sal Rei, Boavista

Time

Cape Verde is one hour behind GMT and does not operate daylight savings. When it is 12 noon in Cape Verde, it is 1pm in London, 8am in New York, 3pm in Cape Town, 8am in Toronto, 11pm in Sydney and 1am the following day in Auckland.

Toilets

Use toilets in hotels and restaurants, which are usually kept in good order. The toilets at large petrol stations are locked but you can ask for the key at the till to use them.

Travellers with disabilities

Hotels in Cape Verde are mainly low rise with steps to walk up to rooms on the second floor. In the big resorts there can be long walks between rooms and restaurants, the pool and other facilities, which are often on several levels. To ensure the hotel is suitable, anyone with mobility problems should inform their travel agent or tour operator of their needs and check access before booking. The cobbled roads and rough tracks make wheelchair use quite difficult and uncomfortable.

Language

The official language in Cape Verde is Portuguese. This is the language of business, education and the media, but you'll hear everyone speaking Crioulo, the fascinating mix of African and Portuguese words that dates back to the days of slavery. English is taught as a second or third language but outside the cities and resorts it helps to have a smattering of Portuguese or French.

Every island has its own version of Crioulo and words and pronunciation can differ widely across the archipelago. The biggest differences are between that spoken in the northern islands (Barlavento Creole) and that of the southern islands (Sotavento Creole). As it is mainly a spoken language, spelling can be idiosyncratic. If you learn and use just a few Crioulo words, it will be much appreciated.

Pronouncing words

x sounds like the English 'sh' in 'shoe'

dj is a 'j' as in 'jug'

tx represents the 'ch' of 'choose' (*txau*, 'goodbye', sounds like the Italian *ciao*)

j is like the 'z' sound in 'pleasure'

k sounds hard, like 'kick'

s is soft as in 'soap'

Useful words and phrases

English	**Krioulo (Santiago)**	**Crioulo (São Vicente)**
Hello	*Oi/Ola*	*Oi*
Goodbye	*Txau*	*Txau*
How's life? (greeting)	*Tudu bon? Tudu dretu?*	*Tud dret? Tud kul?*
Yes	*Sin*	*Sin*
No	*Nau*	*Nau*
Good/fine/cool	*Fixe*	*Kul*
Delicious	*Sabi*	*Sab*
Please	*Pur favor*	*D'favor*
Thank you	*Obrigadu*	*Brigadu*
You're welcome	*Es é ka nada*	*Es ne nada*

English	Krioulo (Santiago)	Crioulo (São Vicente)
Excuse me	*Kon lisensa*	*Kolsensa*
Pardon me/sorry	*Disculpam*	*Dsculpam*
It's all right/not all right	*Sta dretu/Ka sta dretu*	*Ta dret/Ka ta dret*
Do you speak English? (Portuguese? French?)	*Bu tu papia Inglês? (Português? Francês?)*	*Bo ta falá Inglês? (Português? Francês?)*
I don't understand	*N ka ta konprende*	*Un ka intende*
What is your name?	*Mó ki bu tchoma?*	*Mané ke bo nome?*
My name is ...	*Nha nomi ê ...*	*Nha nome ê ...*
How are you?	*Modi ki bu sta?*	*Ke mane bo stâ?*
Why?	*Pamódi?*	*Purque?*
When?	*Kuandu?*	*Kondé?*
Who?	*Ken?*	*Ken?*
Can you help me?	*Bu pode djuda-m?*	*Bo podé jdame?*
Where is the shop/bank?	*Undi ki e loja/banku?*	*Ondé k'e loja/bonk?*
Do you have bottled water?	*Nhos tem agu di garafa?*	*Bzot tem agua d'garafa?*
How much is it?	*Keli e kantu?*	*Keli tonté?*
Could I have a menu?	*Traze'm ementa, pur favor*	*Traze'm imenta, d'favor*
I don't eat meat	*N ka ta kumé karni*	*N ka ta k'mé karn*

English	Portuguese
Good morning	*Bom dia*
Good night	*Boa noite*
How are you?	*Como estás?/tudo bem?*
Tea	*Chá*
Coffee with milk	*Café com leite*
Water	*Água*
White wine	*Vinho branco*
Red wine	*Vinho tinto*
Beer	*Cerveja*
Glass	*Copo*
The bill	*A conta*
Chemist	*Farmácia*
Market	*Mercado*

Emergencies

Emergency telephone numbers

Hospital *130*
Fire *131*
Police *132*

Health

Medical services

Although each island has a hospital, facilities are limited and they may not be able to deal with serious cases of ill health. There's a big hospital in Praia (*Hospital Dr Agostinho Neto. Tel: 260 1010*). Sal's hospital is in Espargos (*Tel: 241 1130*), and is rather basic. The best clinics and hospitals are in Mindelo, São Vicente:
Baptista de Sousa Hospital. Tel: 231 1879/2122/2424.
Urgimed (drop-in private clinic). Tel: 230 0170.
Dental clinic (private). Tel: 230 0087.
Hospital treatment is either free or low cost. Private doctors should be paid, in cash, at the time of consultation. Medical insurance is essential, because serious illness will require evacuation to a country with good facilities.

Health risks

No special vaccinations are required for Cape Verde. Unlike mainland West Africa, malaria is not a problem, although it can occur on Santiago between September and December. The dry climate keeps the biting insect population down but flies can be a real nuisance, especially during the rainy season.

Pack a small medical kit with painkillers, plasters, antiseptic, insect repellent, a treatment for diarrhoea and sachets of oral rehydration salts. Heat exhaustion and stomach upsets are common in tropical countries. Always wear sunblock during the day and cover up. Even when it's cloudy the sun is very strong and you can quickly burn.

Drink bottled water and eat fruit that you've peeled yourself. Avoid ice and ice cream and only eat lobster and seafood in season. Always try to eat hot, freshly prepared food, and wash your hands well before eating.

Crime

The crime rate is low and most visits to Cape Verde are trouble-free. However, this is a poor country and opportunistic theft and muggings do happen, especially in Mindelo and Praia. It is wise to keep an eye on your belongings, and don't wear expensive jewellery or carry large amounts of cash. Streets are not well lit, so be aware of your surroundings and ideally take a taxi back to your hotel at night, even if it is only a short distance.

For travel and safety information, the Foreign and Commonwealth Office website (*www.fco.gov.uk*) has extensive advice on its 'Know before you go' and 'Travel advice by country' pages.

Embassies

Australia, Canada, New Zealand

There is no Australian, Canadian or New Zealand representation in Cape Verde; the nearest High Commissions are in Pretoria, South Africa.

South Africa

South Africa has an Embassy in Dakar, Senegal.

South African Embassy, Mermoz SUD, Lotissement Ecole de Police, Dakar, Senegal. Tel: (+221) 33 865 1959. www.saesenegal.info

UK

There is no formal British representation in Cape Verde.
The nearest British Embassy is in Dakar, Senegal.

British Embassy, 20 Rue du Docteur Guillet (Boîte Postale 6025), Dakar, Senegal. Tel: (+221) 33 823 7392 and (+221) 33 823 9971. www.britishembassy.gov.uk/Senegal.

In an emergency, the British Honorary Consul in Mindelo, São Vicente, can provide limited assistance.

British Honorary Consul, Shell Cabo Verde Sarl, Avenida Amílcar Cabral CP4, Mindelo, São Vicente. Tel: 232 2830. Email: antonio.a.canuto@scv.sims.com or elisabete.e.soares@scv.simis.com

US

The American embassy is in Praia, Santiago.

Embassy of the United States of America, Rua Abilo Macedo 6, Praia. Tel: 260 8900. www.praia.usembassy.gov

Tourists sensibly keeping in the shade on Chaves beach on Boavista

Directory

Accommodation price guide

Prices are based on a double room per night for two people sharing, with breakfast.

★	Under 3,000CVE
★★	3,000–8,000CVE
★★★	8,000–12,000CVE
★★★★	Over 12,000CVE

Eating out price guide

Prices are based on an average two-course meal for one person, without drinks.

★	Under 900CVE
★★	900–1,200CVE
★★★	1,200–1,600CVE
★★★★	Over 1,600CVE

Opening hours are flexible and these details are only included when considered reliable.

SAL

Santa Maria

ACCOMMODATION

Odjo d'Água Hotel ★★
On a promontory jutting out to sea, the best rooms of this independent hotel are alongside the small but attractive pool set in a terraced garden with sea views. It has a private beach with sun loungers and a tiny beachside 'spa'.
Zona Farolinho. Tel: 242 1414. Fax: 242 1430. www.odjodagua.net

Hotel Morabeza ★★★
With its perfect location by the beach and close to the village, tree-shaded terrace and speciality restaurant, attractive bars, pool and plentiful but low-key entertainment, this independent is one of the best hotels on the archipelago. The stylishly upgraded rooms and suites are calm and spacious.
Praia de Santa Maria. Tel: 242 1020. Fax: 242 1005. www.hotelmorabeza.com

Crioula Hotel ★★★★
An Italian club hotel with a health and beauty centre, right on the beach, about a 20-minute walk from Santa Maria village. Accommodation is either in the two-storey wings of the main building, which has restaurants and a few shops, or in the gardens in bungalow-style rooms. The 242 rooms have air conditioning and a furnished balcony or terrace. The big swimming pool, with a thatched bar at the centre, has a children's area. Supervised children's mini club (age three to ten).
Praia de Santa Maria. Tel: 242 1615. Fax: 242 1376. Email: crioulahotel@cvtelecom.cv

Djadsal Holiday Club ★★★★
In front of the beach, about a ten-minute walk

from Santa Maria village. Another Italian holiday club with good facilities and entertainment for families, it has Moorish-style architecture and a swimming pool as the focal point. Good for people who want to dive as Caboverde Diving has a base there.
Praia de Santa Maria. Tel: 242 1170. Fax: 242 1070.

Riu Funana-Garopa ★★★★
Surrounded by high Moorish-style walls, these sister all-inclusive hotels have buffet restaurants, bars, pools, a children's club and organised entertainment. About 2km (1¼ miles) from Santa Maria village.
Riu Funana, Cabocan Lote A2, A3. Tel: 242 9060. Fax: 242 9088. Riu Garopa, Cabocan Lote A2, A3. Tel: 242 9040. Fax: 242 9041. www.riu.com

Eating out

Compad ★★
Friendly little Cape Verdean restaurant serving mainly fish and seafood.
Rua 1 de Janeiro. Tel: 242 1228. Open: lunch & dinner.

Papaya ★★
All day toasties, jacket potatoes and pizzas, surrounded by the sea. Fast Internet, too.
At the Porto Antigo apartments, next to the Odjo d'Água Hotel. Tel: 983 3482.

Ao Caranguejo ★★★
A small wrought-iron gate leads into an inviting courtyard and there is a great traditional Italian menu.
Next to Surf+Soul on Rua 1 de Janeiro. Tel: 997 1216.

Café Cultura ★★★
There are outdoor tables on the main square and it is always busy. The menu includes Creole, European and some nicely spicy dishes. Good value.
Praça. Tel: 995 2646. Open: daily, 10am–midnight.

Cretcheu ★★★
Fish, pizza and pasta on a terrace with views straight out to sea.
By the jetty. Tel: 242 1068. Open: lunch & dinner.

Farolim ★★★
Surrounded by the sea, open to the ocean breeze, the Odjo d'Água Hotel's restaurant is one of the most popular spots on the island. Cape Verdean and European food with live music in the evening.
Zona Farolinho. Tel: 242 1414. www.odjodagua.net

Funaná ★★★
Rustic bar and restaurant in African-style *rondavels* on the beach, famed for its 'Roda Creola' Cape Verdean night buffets and live music.
On the beach, near Hotel Morabeza. Tel: 242 1238. www.restaurantefunana.com. Open: bar 9am–midnight, kitchen noon–3pm & 8–10pm.

Americo's ★★★★
Fish and meat dishes are on the menu of this first-floor restaurant that's almost always packed. Live music after 10pm.
Rua 1 de Janeiro. Tel: 242 1011. Open: lunch & dinner.

Beach Club, Hotel Morabeza ★★★★
Right on the beach, an elegantly relaxed bar and restaurant serving superb food with endless beach

and sea views.
Praia de Santa Maria. Tel: 242 1020. www.hotelmorabeza.com. Open: lunch only.

Chez Pastis ★★★★
Small Italian restaurant tucked into a narrow passageway. Delicious, imaginative food, lovely atmosphere. Must book.
Rua Amílcar Cabral. Tel: 984 3696. Open: dinner. Closed: Sun.

Restaurante Atlantis ★★★★
Cape Verdean, Italian and French cuisine with terraces on the beach. The daily lunch menu specials are cheap. There is live music four nights a week.
In the Center Atlantis, in front of the Hotel Belorizonte. Tel: 242 1879. Open: noon– 4.30pm & after 6pm.

Entertainment

Bar Calema
Local and international music, live on Fridays. Serves up one of the best *caipirinhas* in town.
Rua 1 de Janeiro. Open: 5pm–2am.

Chill-Out Bar
Laidback bar with a sports screen and a terrace on the street for people-watching. International sounds, local live music, serves snacks.
Rua 1 de Janeiro. Open: late afternoon–2am.

Pirata Disco
Theme nights, lively at weekends after midnight. Rap, hip-hop, Cape Verdean and Latin American sounds.
At the entrance to Santa Maria by the airport road. Admission charge.

Q Bar
On the terrace right beside the sea at the Odjo d'Água Hotel.
Zona Farolinho. Tel: 242 1400.

Roots Bar
Lively African-influenced bar, open at night.
Rua 1 de Janeiro.

Tam Tam
Popular with British tourists and expats, Irish-run bar and restaurant that screens international matches.
Rua Amílcar Cabral. Open: 8am–12.30am.

Sport and leisure

Angulo Cape Verde Windsurf Centre
Run by windsurfing world champion Josh Angulo, the centre has a large selection of Ezzy Sails and Angulo boards.
On the southeast end of Santa Maria beach near the Sab-Sab Hotel. Email: joshangulo@angulocaboverde.com. www.angulocaboverde.com. Open: end Oct–end June.

Barracuda Tours
Barracuda Tours can organise excursions, book inter-island flights and arrange guided tours of Sal or any of the Cape Verde islands. They have offices in Santa Maria, at Sal airport and also on Boavista, São Vicente and Santiago.
Edifício Barracuda, Rua 1 Julho. Tel: 242 2033. Fax: 242 2029. www.barracudatours.com

Cabo Verde Diving
Established and well-equipped dive company with a good reputation. Multi-lingual staff. A range of PADI courses.
At Hotel Djadsal and Hotel Crioula, Praia

de Santa Maria. Tel: 997 8824. www. caboverdediving.net

Cabo Verde Fishing Center

Deep sea, trawling and big game blue marlin fishing trips. Quad bikes to take you surf casting.

Centro Atlantis. Tel/fax: 993 1332. Email: caboverdefishingcenter@yahoo.it. www. caboverdefishingcenter.com

Neptunus

The 'yellow submarine' runs morning and night trips to watch underwater life and see shipwrecks from its viewing chamber.

At the jetty, Santa Maria. Tel: 999 4200.

Quad hire

Escorted quad biking on the sands and dunes. Book at the Hotel Morabeza activities desk.

Praia de Santa Maria. Tel: 242 1020.

Rent Bike

Cycle hire, Internet and low-cost Internet phone calls.

IP Net, Entrada Santa Maria. Tel: 242 2069. Open: Mon–Fri 9am–12.30pm & 4–7.30pm, Sat 9am–12.30pm.

Sal Sport Fishing

Big game fishing from a 10m (33ft) boat. Go for grouper, tuna, sailfish or blue marlin.

By the jetty. Tel: 999 1062. www.salsportfishing.com

Surf Zone

Run by some of the best kite surfers, windsurfers and surfers on Sal, Surf Zone has the latest equipment for hire at all levels. Small group or individual lessons by multilingual instructors.

On the beach next to the Morabeza Beach Club. Tel: 997 8804. www. surfcaboverde.com. www. kitesurfcaboverde.com

BOAVISTA

Espingueira

Accommodation

Spinguera ★★★★

The ultimate get-away-from-it-all retreat. Eco-hotel on a deserted coast designed with pure Italian style. Just 12 beautifully appointed rooms in small stone houses, fresh Cape Verdean and creative Mediterranean cuisine, a cosy library and bar. All meals and airport transfers are included in the price.

Tel: 999 1021. www.spinguera.com

Rabil

Accommodation

Parque das Dunas Village ★★★

Right on spectacular Chaves beach, a small hotel with simply furnished, bungalow-style rooms reached by a cobbled path in gardens of tropical plants. Stunning pool, alfresco restaurant and bar. No air conditioning (there are fans) and no phones or television in the rooms. Very relaxing.

Praia de Chaves. Tel: 251 1288. Fax: 251 1339. www. parquedasdunas.com

Sal Rei

Accommodation

Migrante ★★

Pretty yellow and blue colonial-style guesthouse in the heart of Sal Rei, with stylishly comfortable rooms, a courtyard and attractive bar with live music. Breakfast and

airport transfer included in the price.
Avenida Amílcar Cabral. Tel/fax: 251 1143. www.migrante-guesthouse.com

Estoril Beach Resort Hotel ★★★
About a ten-minute walk from the centre of Sal Rei, and not far from the beach, this is an attractive hotel with bright and cheerful rooms built around a courtyard with a Spanish flavour. Apartments are also available. Italian-style restaurant and a bar that serves lunch snacks.
Praia Estoril. Tel: 251 1078. Fax: 251 1046. www.estorilbeachresort.com

Hotel Dunas ★★★★
A bright hotel along the seafront with an umbrella-shaded terrace restaurant. Guests can use the water-sports and sunlounger facilities on Tortuga beach, about a five-minute walk away.
Avenida Amílcar Cabral. Tel: 251 1225. Fax: 251 1384. Email: dunas.boavista@gmail.com

Eating out

Il Capriccio ★
Terrific fresh Italian pasta with a huge choice of sauces in a light and airy, white-walled setting. There is a children's menu, too.
Localidade Ribeirinha. Tel: 999 1906. Open: 8.30am–midnight.

Bar-Restaurante Rosy ★★
In an orange house with brown wooden shutters, offering the freshest of fresh food cooked to order. Famous for lobster dishes. Reserve by 10am for lunch, midday for dinner.
Avenida Amílcar Cabral. Tel: 251 1242. Open: lunch & dinner.

Blue Marlin ★★
Tiny bar-restaurant on the main square. Great fish (the owner is a big game fisherman) and friendly atmosphere. Book in advance.
Praça. Tel: 992 3871. Open: lunch & dinner.

Restaurante Naida ★★
Family-run restaurant serving grilled fish, chicken and goat. Book in advance.
Praça, near the church. Tel: 251 1173. Open: lunch & dinner.

Terra Sabe ★★
Serving Cape Verdean and Italian dishes on an upstairs terrace, with pork and chicken options as well as fish.
Behind the Nazarene church. Tel: 993 9078. Open: Mon–Sat 10am–midnight & Sun 7pm–midnight.

Sport and leisure

Boavista Wind Club
The latest sails and boards, windsurfing and kite surfing lessons. Run by world champion François Guy.
On Tortuga beach. Email: boavista012@yahoo.com. www.boavistawindclub.com

Dive School Submarine Centre
Two qualified diving instructors run their operation from a cargo-ship container near the harbour. PADI and NAUI (National Association of Underwater Instructors) courses, snorkelling and dives from their Zodiac boat.
Tel: 992 7866. Email: atilros@hotmail.com

Quadland Boavista
Scooter rent and guided

quad excursions across the endless sands and dunes. Book through hotels or from the office on the main square.
Praça. www.quadland-boavista.com. Open: Mon–Sat 9am–6.30pm.

SÃO VICENTE

Mindelo

Accommodation

Residencial Che Guevara ★★
A welcoming guesthouse near Laginha beach and close to town, with ten adequate rooms, a restaurant, bar and Internet facilities.
6 Avenida Che Guevara. Tel: 232 2449. Fax: 232 4265. http://res_cheguevara.tripod.com

Residencial Jenny ★★
There are fabulous views over Mindelo Bay from the balcony rooms of this small hotel in a historic residential district close to town and the port. It has 20 rooms, a garden, breakfast room, lounge and Internet facilities.
Alto São Nicolau. Tel: 232 8969. Fax: 232 3939. Email: hstaubyn@cvtelecom.cv

Porto Grande Oásis Atlântico Hotel ★★★
On the Praça Nova in the heart of town, so convenient for the restaurants and nightlife of Mindelo, a friendly international hotel with restaurant, bar, café, gym and swimming pool.
Praça Amílcar Cabral. Tel: 232 3190. Fax: 232 3193. www.oasisatlantico.com

Eating out

Café Algarve ★
Terrace café opposite the Presidential Palace. Light meals and drinks all day, live music some nights.
Rua de Lisboa.

Café Lisboa ★
Tiny café for your midday gin and tonic among some of Mindelo's most interesting characters. Snacks and a great atmosphere.
Rua de Lisboa.

Restaurante Chaves d'Oures ★
Don't let the dingy entrance to this *pensão* put you off. Upstairs there's an airy, high-ceilinged restaurant of colonial heritage with potted ferns and lace tablecloths. Good, inexpensive food overlooking Rua Lisboa.
Corner of Avenida 5 de Julho and Rua Lisboa. Tel: 232 7050.

Restaurante Archote ★★
Cool breezes flow among the plants at this terraced restaurant. Cape Verdean fish dishes and seafood are the specialities. Live music in the evenings towards the end of the week.
Rua Irmãs Amor Deus, Alto São Nicolau. Tel: 232 3916. Open: lunch & dinner.

Restaurante Cafeteria Gaudí ★★
Pleasant restaurant in the heart of town. Inexpensive *menu do dia* at lunchtime.
Off Rua de Lisboa, opposite the side entrance to the market. Tel: 232 7799. Open: daily.

Nella's ★★★
Steep stairs lead to a relaxed restaurant and bar on the first floor, with a balcony overlooking Rua Lisboa. Famed for fish, but the meat's very good too. European in style and

décor. Great atmosphere and memorable live music. A Mindelo favourite.
Rua de Lisboa. Tel: 231 4320.

Tradisson e Morabeza ★★★★
Mindelo's smartest restaurant looks out over the harbour. Cape Verdean and Mediterranean dishes on the menu. Live music Mon–Sat 11pm–3am.
Rua d'Praia, near the Belem Tower. Tel: 232 4841. Open: 8pm until late.

Entertainment

Acid Movement
Disco close to Syrius (*see below*). Plays loud rock, electro and pop, plus there's a basement bar lounge.
Tucked away in a tiny street behind the old Eden Park cinema on Praça Nova (turn right by the church to find the street). Open: Fri & Sat, sometimes Thur. Admission charge.

Le Café Musique
Busy bar owned by the brilliant guitarist, Bau.
Rua de Lisboa.

Jazzy Birds
Popular pre-clubbing bar offers DVDs, zouk, pop and traditional music.
Rua de Cavaquinho.

Mindel Hotel
Live music in the bar at weekends and regular nightclub concerts.
Avenida 5 de Julho. Tel: 232 8882.

Syrius
Easily recognised by the wall sculptures outside, this nightclub is attached to the Porto Grande Hotel on Praça Nova. A young crowd dance to zouk and kuduro. Always packed on Friday and Saturday nights.
Just off Praça Amílcar Cabral. Admission charge.

Tabuh
Bar in the same street as Syrius (*see above*). Big screen, good cocktails.

Sport and leisure

Sport Fishing
With Didier Jeanne aboard his Bertram 33 boat *Nha Cretcheu*. The channel between São Vicente and Santo Antão is famous for blue marlin, and catches of 200–300kg (440–660lb) are common.
Residencial Alto Fortim, Alto Fortim. Tel: 995 1546. Fax: 232 3936. www. pechesportivecapvert.com

São Pedro

Accommodation

Hotel Foya Branca ★★★
Resort hotel by São Pedro beach and near the airport. Large rooms, suites and villas with sea and garden views, swimming pool, children's facilities, restaurants and bars. Windsurfing, tennis, bike and car hire, and sport fishing available. Free shuttle bus transport into Mindelo town 10km (6 miles) away.
Praia de São Pedro. Tel: 230 7400. Fax: 230 7444. www.foyabranca.com

Sport and leisure

Blue Discovery
Watersports centre with PADI diving, deep sea fishing, snorkelling, wind and body board surfing.
Hotel Foya Branca.

Tel: 997 7168.
www.bluediscovery.com

SANTO ANTÃO

Ponta do Sol

Accommodation

Por De Sol Arte ★
Overlooking the sea, this French-run guesthouse has seven rooms.
Near the harbour.
Tel: 255 1121.

Hotel Blue Bell ★★
Modern hotel on the main square with 24 rooms looking out to the mountains or the sea.
Praça. Tel: 225 1215.

Eating out

NB: All restaurants in Ponta do Sol require you to phone in advance to order.

A Beira Mar ★★
Light and prettily decorated in gold and blue, this restaurant is close to the harbour.
Tel: 225 1008. Open: Mon–Sat lunch & dinner, Sun dinner only.

Cretcheu di Mar ★★
Fish and chicken are the daily lunch menu basics in this pleasant restaurant in the Hotel Blue Bell, with tables overlooking the Town Hall and church on the main square.
Praça. Tel: 225 1215.

Oveleiro ★★
Fish restaurant and bar on the rocks by the harbour.
Tel: 225 1490.

Por d'Sol ★★
'Restaurante panoramico chez Ba' with charming sea-marine décor, overlooking the harbour.
Tel: 992 0417. Open: lunch & dinner.

Sport and leisure

Cabo Verde Bikes
Rents bikes, organises tours and treks, sells crafts and local produce, and can rustle up a tasty pizza while you're planning. Owner André Szpera believes tourism must involve local people and he is a mine of information.
On the wide street leading from the harbour to the Praça at Ponta do Sol.
Tel: 255 1526 & 982 5059.
www.cabo-verde-bikes.com

Ribeira Grande

Accommodation

Pedracin Village ★★
Eco-retreat in the mountains, a 15-minute drive from Ribeira Grande. There are ten stone-built cottages (20 rooms) built into the rock. The retreat is part of a farm and the vegetables and fruit are home grown, solar power heats the water, and the views from the terrace bar, restaurant and swimming pool are spectacular.
Boca Coruja. Tel: 224 2020. Email: pedracin@cvtelecom.cv

SANTIAGO

Cidade Velha

Eating out

Casinha Velha ★
Small restaurant on the main square; its owner trained as a chef in Germany.
Rua de Calhau.
Tel: 267 3135.

Praia

Accommodation

Hotel Pestana Tropico ★★★
Overlooking the ocean in Prainha, the city's suburb of diplomatic residences, the spacious rooms surround a large sea-water pool. Used by both business and leisure

travellers, it has a circular bar and the restaurant 'Alex' has a high reputation. On three levels, with no lift, it is not suitable for families.
Cidade da Praia Prainha. Tel: 261 4200. Fax: 261 5225. www.pestana.com

Hotel Praia Mar Oásis Atlântico ★★★
Large resort-style hotel overlooking a beach and the sea in Prainha. Restaurant, poolside coffee shop, children's pool, gym with sauna and jacuzzi, floodlit tennis, nightclub, and Avis car rental desk.
Cidade da Praia Prainha. Tel: 261 4153. Fax: 261 2972. www.oasisatlantico.com

Eating out

Alkimist ★★
Bar and lounge. Pizzas, pastas and music in the evenings.
On the beach at Quebra Canela. Tel: 262 4826.

Beramar Grill ★★★
Watch your fish being grilled to perfection on the outdoor grill.
Below the Moura Bus Company building by the sea in Chã d'Areia. Tel: 261 6400.

Churrasqueira Dragoeiro ★★★
Barbecues and shish kebabs. Very popular at weekends.
Opposite the Ministry of Justice, Achada Santo António. Tel: 262 3335.

Plaza Park ★★★
Grilled fish, seafood and traditional dishes, close to the Parliament building in Achada Santo António.
Tel: 262 1080. Open: lunch & dinner.

Gamboa ★★★★
Much favoured by government ministers and visiting dignitaries.
Avenida Oua, Chã d'Areia. Tel: 261 2008.

O Poeta ★★★★
One of Praia's best and most popular restaurants with views over the harbour and live music in the evenings.
In the Embassy area of Achada Santo António. Tel: 261 3800.

Entertainment

A Capital
Nightclub in the Hotel Praia Mar complex, busy at weekends.
Prainha. Tel: 261 4153.

Quintal da Música
Founded by members of the popular group Simentera to promote traditional Cape Verdean music, this venue has a courtyard stage.
Avenida Amílcar Cabral, Plâto. Tel: 261 7282. Open: Mon–Sat. Closed: Sun.

Rui Vaz

Accommodation

Quinta da Montanha ★★
Up in the Rui Vaz mountains, this family-run rural retreat specialises in eco- and agro-tourism. Part of a working farm, it grows organic crops for its rooftop restaurant.
Rui Vaz. Tel: 268 5002 & 992 4013. Email: quintamontanha@cvtelecom.cv

Tarrafal

Eating out

Baía Verde ★★★
Restaurant overlooking the beach. Traditional dishes including fish, goat stew, grilled chicken and *cachupa* (stew).
Complexo Turístico Baía Verde, Tarrafal. Tel: 262 1128.

FOGO

Chã das Caldeiras

Accommodation

Pousada Pedra Brabo ★
In the heart of the volcano, an amazing place with simple rooms, good food and great views. Restaurant open to non-residents.
Vulcão. Tel: 282 1521, 982 6043. Fax: 261 2904. Email: pedrabrabo@cvtelecom.cv. www.pedrabrabo.net

São Filipe

Accommodation

Pousada Belavista ★★
Attractive guesthouse in the heart of São Filipe, with courtyard rooms in traditional *sobrado* (mansion) style.
Achada Pato. Tel: 281 1734. Fax: 281 1879. Email: p_belavista@yahoo.com

Hotel Xaguate ★★★
Fogo's only hotel of an international standard has a good restaurant and tempting pool in gardens with an ocean view.
CP47, on the edge of town. Tel: 281 5000. Fax: 281 1203. Email: xaguate@cvtelecom.cv

Eating out

Le Bistrot ★
Spacious outside terrace and a cheerfully attractive interior. Good for fish and pizza.
Baixo da Igreja. Tel: 984 5875. Open: lunch & dinner.

Maria Amélia Pensão Bar Restaurante ★
Boasts 'the best food in town' at the upstairs terrace restaurant. Live music during the week.
Rua do Mercado, opposite the market. Tel: 991 9929. Open: lunch & dinner.

Restaurante Seafood Bar ★
Panoramic sea views, but not a lot of seafood.
Overlooking the beach. Tel: 283 1045.

Pensão Las Vegas ★★
Restaurant and bar on an open-air terrace that serves food all day (unusual in Cape Verde).
Achada Pato. Tel: 281 1281.

Entertainment

Club Esplanade
Bar, restaurant and nightclub next to the Cape Cod restaurant.
Tel: 281 1820.

Tropical Club
Leafy courtyard restaurant and Internet café by day turns disco at night, with traditional music on Friday.
Achada Pato, near the TACV office. Tel: 281 2161.

SÃO NICOLAU

Ribeira Brava

Accommodation

Pensão Residencial Jardim ★
B&B perched on the hillside with lovely views.
Chãzinha. Tel: 235 1117. Fax: 235 1949.

Pensão Santos & Santos ★
B&B on a square at the south end of town.
Estância Baixo. Tel: 235 1830.

Pensão Santo António ★★
Friendly guesthouse overlooking the main square; pleasant rooms.
Terreiro. Tel: 235 2200. Fax: 235 2199.

Eating out

Restaurante Bar Bela Sombra Dalila ★
One of the best places to eat in Ribeira Brava. Good fish and chicken.
Estância Baixo, near the church. Tel: 235 1831. Open: lunch & dinner.

Index

Acknowledgements

Thomas Cook Publishing wishes to thank SUE DOBSON for the photographs in this book, to whom the copyright belongs, except for the following images:

BARRACUDA TOURS 131, 132a & b, 133
CABO VERDE DIVING 134
HOLIDAY OPTIONS 112
WIKIMEDIA COMMONS/Matt Edmonds 113

The author would like to thank Alan Brown of Holiday Options and Romina Carneiro of Barracuda Tours, and their teams, for their invaluable assistance in organising the research trip involved in the preparation of this book.

For CAMBRIDGE PUBLISHING MANAGEMENT LTD:

Project editor: Rosalind Munro
Copy editor: Joanne Osborn
Typesetter: Trevor Double
Proofreader: Jenni Rainford
Indexer: Karolin Thomas

SEND YOUR THOUGHTS TO BOOKS@THOMASCOOK.COM

We're committed to providing the very best up-to-date information in our travel guides and constantly strive to make them as useful as they can be. You can help us to improve future editions by letting us have your feedback. If you've made a wonderful discovery on your travels that we don't already feature, if you'd like to inform us about recent changes to anything that we do include, or if you simply want to let us know your thoughts about this guidebook and how we can make it even better – we'd love to hear from you.

Send us ideas, discoveries and recommendations today and then look out for your valuable input in the next edition of this title.

Emails to the above address, or letters to Travellers Series Editor, Thomas Cook Publishing, PO Box 227, Unit 9, Coningsby Road, Peterborough PE3 8SB, UK.

Please don't forget to let us know which title your feedback refers to!